THE MAP

By Gordon Adair

Published by Compass-Publishing UK
ISBN 978-1-915962-37-9

Acknowledgements

My thanks go to everyone who contributed to this book. For some, it was the first time they had ever told their story and I know how difficult and draining that can be.

I hope I have not let you down.

I would also like to put on record my thanks to the man who first gave me a copy of the map, since when he has worked tirelessly to open doors for me, helping and encouraging others to tell their stories, something they felt unable to do for many years.

Thanks also to Greg at Hardlight, to Lorna Quin and my sister Vanessa for their proof-reading skills and to my family for their encouragement and patience.

Cover artwork design by Greg Haire
Book layout, design & printing by Greg Haire & Peter Haire of Hardlight Multimedia, Glenanne, Co. Armagh
(www.hardlight.net)

© Copyright 2024 - All rights reserved.
No part of this publication may be reproduced, copied or transmitted in any form or by any means, without the permission of the author.

A copy of this book is contained in the British Library.

For Ian and Dennis who both made it home safely – and for all the fathers who didn't.

The Map

Foreword

By Danny Kennedy

I am delighted and honoured to provide a foreword to this important book by my good friend and distinguished Northern Ireland broadcaster and journalist, Gordon Adair.

I believe this book will enable all those who read it to better understand the huge issues and problems faced by the security forces in South Armagh during the period of "The Troubles" as they battled to maintain law and order in the area known as "Bandit Country".

As someone brought up in South Armagh and who continues to live there, I am deeply familiar with the challenges faced by security personnel throughout that dark period. I salute the bravery and courage shown by all those who served in the security forces. I also believe it is important that their service and sacrifice should be recognised and remembered by the wider community and indeed nationally and internationally.

The stories in this book have been carefully and painstakingly chosen by the author, using detailed interviews and research material with now retired members of the security forces, mostly RUC personnel. In my view, Gordon has captured very graphically their lived experiences of heroism, raw courage and danger without in any way seeking to sensationalise or glorify these factual accounts.

Gordon Adair is a much respected journalist and broadcaster. He has faced and battled with significant health issues over many years and has rightly won the admiration of family, friends and professional colleagues as a result.

I believe this book is important because it enables some of the genuine heroes of the bitter and bloody conflict of that period to tell their story and set the record straight. It will therefore be an essential resource to those who want to better understand and study, not only the horrendous events we endured in this area of Northern Ireland, but also the price so many paid in their efforts to protect the entire community from the barbarism of those dark days.

Danny Kennedy

November 2023.

Danny Kennedy is a Welfare Support Officer with The Ely Centre which provides support and assistance to victims and survivors of The Troubles including security force personnel. He was previously an elected representative for the Newry & Armagh constituency in the NI Assembly, serving also as Minister for Regional Development.

THE MAP

By Gordon Adair

About The Author

Gordon Adair is an award-winning journalist. He was born, raised and educated in Armagh. His first job in journalism was with the Portadown Times before moving to the News Letter and Daily Mirror.

He joined the BBC in 2000 and spent more than two decades as the corporation's regional reporter in Armagh, South Tyrone and South Down.

He still lives in County Armagh with his wife, two daughters, dog and part-time cat. This is his first book.

For further information visit his website:

www.gordonadair.com

CONTENTS

Introduction 1

Before The Deluge 9

Ballgowns and Blood Trails..19

Rubber Bounces Back 37

Mortars 47

Sniper 59

Massacre 71

Blue on Blue...85

The Detective 99

A Matter of Life and Death 117

Split Second 129

White Lines 135

The 'On Switch' 145

The Price Of Peace Is Eternal Vigilance 151

Ghosts.. 165

Bibliography 173

The Map

Introduction

For almost three decades, right at the centre of one of the most secretive places in Northern Ireland, the Joint Operations Planning Room for South Armagh, there was a huge map.

It showed the rugged, hilly terrain of what was then, if you were a British soldier or a police officer, the most dangerous posting in the world; a place that was hard to know, harder still to hold.

But the map also showed the names of every victim of the Northern Ireland conflict in this, its most infamous killing ground as well as the exact location where they had died.

The security base where the map was situated was in a converted 19th century linen mill in the 'Model' village of Bessbrook. From a highly restricted area within it, senior police and military officers planned and co-ordinated the war against the IRA at its most dangerous, its most ruthless, its most brutally efficient. This was the IRA's home ground; this was so-called 'Bandit Country'.

The decisions taken in this room could, and most probably would, mean the difference between life and death. Carelessness could kill, bad luck could kill. And the map, with its coldly efficient recording of every violent death, would never let you forget that.

A Chinook helicopter at Bessbrook Mill which was the busiest
helicopter base in Europe during The Troubles
Photo: John Davis

It was Northern Ireland secretary Merlyn Rees who first coined the phrase "Bandit Country" in the mid 70s. The impression he gave, quite deliberately, was of a barely civilised, lawless place apart. Those who lived there didn't like the term. Nor did those who worked there. To the police, it was the less emotive "Newry subdivision", to the military it was the coldly clinical "NIBAT1" (Northern Ireland Battalion One).

Policing in this area was unlike *anywhere* else. The Constable with a summons to serve in England maybe brought a bicycle; in Crossmaglen, he brought a semi-automatic rifle, 36 soldiers, three helicopters and the hi-tech surveillance capabilities of a network of watchtowers.

A military 'Wessex' helicopter brings supplies to an Army observation post, one of 10 such installations strung along the border with the Irish Republic.

Across the top of the map, a strap-line read: 'The Price of Terrorism'. For those with the security clearance to be in that office, it may as well have read: 'The Price of Failure'. This was a pressure cooker environment where hyper-vigilance was the default setting and courage and resilience were tested to their breaking points.

The map, like all security apparatus, was removed from Bessbrook Mill as the army and police left for the final time at the end of June 2007. By then, there were 316 names on it, 316 dots, representing men, women and children whose lives had been ended prematurely by the violence that engulfed this corner of the island of Ireland, this small part of the United Kingdom, for 30 years.

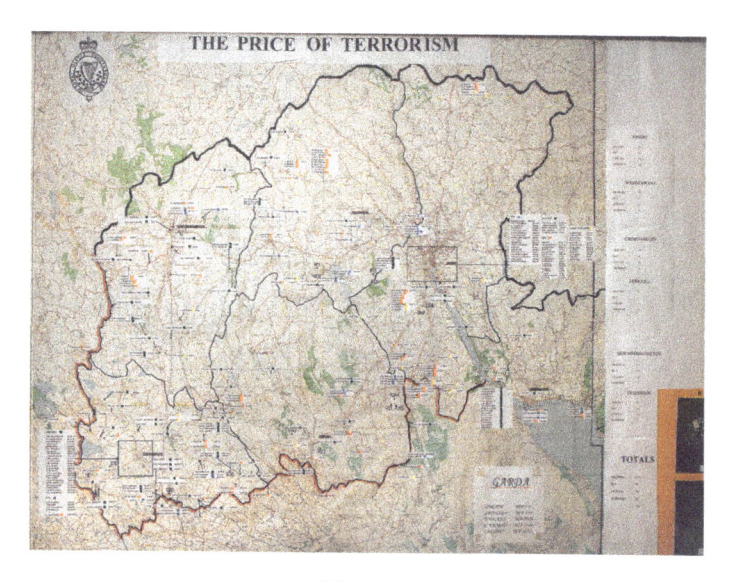

The Map

Many of those killed are remembered now only by family and perhaps a few friends. Time, relentless and irretrievable, reduces that number still further year on year.

Others died in incidents so horrific and savage that they are burned permanently into the consciousness of all of us who are old enough to remember them; Kingsmills, Darkley, Tullyvallen. The list goes on.

The same period also saw over 1,250 bomb attacks in this area of less than 200 square miles and a similar number of shooting incidents.

Yet convictions for IRA-related activity in South Armagh were rare to say the least.

It's not the purpose or intention of this book to attempt to reinterpret the long and complicated history of the IRA. That has been done comprehensively by many writers whose knowledge of that organisation far outstrips mine.

It is, however, important for the reader to get an idea of just how different the South Armagh 'Brigade' was from the rest of the Republican movement.

From the mid-70s onwards, the 'old guard' leadership of the IRA was gradually pushed out by a younger faction. This new generation would go on to restructure the organisation around a newly-created Northern Command and so-called active service units (ASUs).

The ASUs operated as independent cells. Volunteers would have known the handful of people in their own ASU; nothing more. There was, therefore, no risk of them giving away huge amounts of information were they to be 'turned' or arrested and interrogated. They would be much more secure than the leaky 'battalion' structure. At least, that was the theory. The reality was not quite so clear-cut.

But there was another reason for the restructure. The younger generation had accepted that the early military victory, which had seemed possible to some Republicans at the very start of the 70s, was simply not going to happen. The ASU/cell structure was much better suited to the "long war" that they now envisaged; the approach that Sinn Fein's director of publicity, Danny Morrison, would later describe as "the Armalite and the ballot box".

The ONLY place where the restructure did not happen was South Armagh. It simply wasn't needed. South Armagh retained its 'brigade' structure with two 'battalions', one based around Jonesboro, the other at Crossmaglen and continued to prosecute a campaign that was the closest the IRA ever came to conventional warfare.

The changes were simply not needed. The South Armagh Brigade was believed to be virtually leakproof (although we now know this was not entirely true), mostly self-funding, highly motivated and seemingly without mercy.

When a 'tout' WAS discovered, the punishment was almost invariably death, but death in a most cruel, humiliating and highly visible way. The image, once seen, of bound, partially stripped, often hooded, bodies dumped on lonely backroads is nigh on impossible to erase. These deaths too appeared on the map, these deaths too had to be dealt with by the RUC, these deaths too added to the psychological burden carried by those who served in these beautiful, but blood-soaked borderlands.

The IRA in South Armagh operated differently from the rest of the organisation.

Police officers and soldiers lived in constant fear of attacks like this one in 1981. Five soldiers were killed in this attack when their Saracen armoured vehicle drove over a massive land mine.

As we have slowly emerged from the morass of the 'Troubles', much has been said, and continues to be said, about legacy and reconciliation. One of the trickiest, and at times most divisive, challenges has been how to define a 'victim'. All the victims, bar one, I have written about in this book were or are police officers. This is NOT to suggest, in any way, that RUC lives were somehow more valuable than any others or to forget that 258 of the 316 deaths recorded on the map were not police officers.

But policing was, and is, an important part of the South Armagh story and that of the wider 'Troubles'. For many of those who have been kind enough to speak to me, this has been the first time they have spoken about their experience, unique as it was, of policing this 'place apart'.

With the simple message "'Skewer-42' you are clear for take-off," the last military helicopter lifted off the ground and flew away from Bessbrook Mill. It was June 22, 2007. A month later the longest operation in the history of the British Army - Operation Banner - was over. It had lasted 37 years.
Photo: John Davis, Bessbrook, June 22, 2007.

My sincere hope is that the accounts contained here will make a contribution to our overall understanding of a dark period in our history, one we must all hope is never repeated.

The Map

1

Before The Deluge

In the south Armagh of 1969, CCTV still seemed like the stuff of science-fiction. Alerted by an unfamiliar sound outside the station, Crossmaglen sergeant 'Drew'* bent his head to bring his eye level with a peephole in the heavy steel gate. As he slid the cover to one side, his field of vision was filled with the chilling sight of armed attackers. They were dressed in fatigues, carrying rifles and apparently trying to detonate a bomb. No help was coming. Drew was in a fight for his life…….

"I suppose for me, the one thought that brings a sense of relief is that nobody under my direct command was ever killed. There's comfort in that." Today, Drew is well into his 80s. But he still cuts an impressive figure; tall and slim with an easy air of authority. Here, in the cosy sitting room of his County Armagh bungalow, we are surrounded by photographs of beloved children and favourite horses. A handsome clock chimes out gentle reminders that the morning is floating away all too quickly on a sea of coffee and memories.

It's a peaceful time in a peaceful house. Only the bulletproof glass – installed long ago – reminds you that it was not always so and that this peace came at a fearful price.

Drew became the station sergeant in Crossmaglen in the late '60s, moving into the married quarters with his wife and six-month-old baby. It was, he says, a happy time in what was just another small country station.

A blind eye was turned to low-level smuggling, a gentle nudge cleared the late-night drinkers from the village's twenty one pubs. Drew recalls: "Often, by the time you got to the last few, you were putting out the same boys you'd just put out of the first few."

By way of transport, the station was equipped with one canvas-topped Land Rover which had been blown up during the IRA campaign of the 1950s.

"They fixed it up and sent it to us," said Drew. "It was ok if you could get it started but most of the time you couldn't. Many's a day the people of the village helped us push it round the Square to try to get it going."

Drew's gundog was "borrowed by half the country", he bought a boat and fished the local loughs, his wife pushed the pram around the village without concern. In many ways, it was an idyllic life.

His affection for the locals is obvious still, although he accepts that many lived off their wits and that things there were done just slightly differently from elsewhere .

"One night, I found a torch sitting on a bridge. In those days a powerful hand torch like that was a desirable item. They were like hen's teeth." It had, he was sure, been abandoned by somebody 'lamping' salmon, a form of poaching. It didn't require much detective work to find the owner; he had written his name and address on the battery. He was called in to the station and allowed to take his torch and go. "A few days later," said Drew, "I found a big salmon, all wrapped in newspaper, sitting on the doorstep of the married quarters. Later, I bumped into the torch's owner and thanked him for it. He smiled and denied any knowledge of it. That was just how things worked."

Right across Northern Ireland, though, everything was changing with a scope and speed that few could have predicted. Before long, Drew's quiet country station would become a virtual byword for insurrection and violence - and he would survive three attempts on his life.

For Drew, that change pivoted around the death, in Armagh, of a young man called John Gallagher. Drew was close by when the 23-year-old Catholic was shot. "I could feel the whole atmosphere change," he says. "It was like a dark cloud coming over everything and I remember thinking 'now the trouble's going to start'."

It was August 14, 1969.

"All but one of us had been sent from Crossmaglen to help out in Armagh that night. We were just up by the entrance to the market off the Cathedral Road. They were rioting like hell down at the corner. Next thing, there was this rattle of rifle fire and the bullets were flying everywhere. It was a group of B Men** from Tynan*** doing the shooting. As it turned out, it was the DI's fault. He rushed out without giving them any instructions other than 'follow me'. And they lost him. When I came down the road, they were surrounded by the crowd. There were shots fired and one of them hit the boy Gallagher.

"So I went back to Crossmaglen thinking things weren't good. I had a contact, I'll not say his name, just across the border at that time. And I was told that something was going to happen. I wasn't told what, but to be on my guard.

"Well, I had a feeling; almost like a premonition. My mother and father were visiting us in Crossmaglen at that time so I sent them home and sent my wife and daughter to my wife's mother's house. That was on the Saturday. On the Sunday night, a dose of B Men were being sent up. They were starting to arrive when I heard a noise outside.

"I looked out through the peephole, and there were the three boys: berets, army fatigues, rifles, the whole lot, sitting in the front of a van ready to get out.

"I ran to the office to get one of the new Sterlings. One of the B Men had grabbed the other and cocked it. He fired it accidentally and six bullets went rattling down the hall, missed me by inches. I could feel the dust hitting me as it flew off the big old plaster wall.

"I looked out again and now there were three boys in the back of the van and one of them was striking matches.

"So I reached for the sterling, stuck in a mag, and cocked it….. only for the butt plate to fall off the back of it!" He was fast running out of options. He pushed the barrel of his revolver through the peephole.

"By this time, the other boys had let the tailgate down and were running away. I fired a shot, didn't hit anybody, but as they ran away one of them threw a hand grenade back at the van. But instead of going in, it rolled under the van and exploded."

Around this time, the Irish army had moved up to and, according to Drew, over the border. "There were two nights when I saw two of the wee Irish army scout cars, they were Renaults I think, you know those little putt putt jobs. I saw them driving past the station and out towards Cullaville. I was tempted to fire at them (they were invading you see) but then I saw a big machine-gun mounted on the front and thought I'd better not."

On another occasion, shots were fired at the 'not-so-trusty' Land Rover from a Thompson submachine gun as they drove along Concession Road****, but they deflected off without causing any injury.

Perhaps Drew's greatest escape, though, happened without a single shot being fired and, once again, it was the people of Crossmaglen who saved him.

He explained: "There was a Protestant family called Hales, and they used to go every Saturday night to the stock cars in Portadown. We got a call to say that Hales' house and hay shed were on fire.

"And I was gathering the men up when I got a phone call from a very well-known gentleman who lived not far away and told me not to go near it for there was an ambush planned. We didn't go. But the next day we went up and we searched the place and we found where they had set up the Bren gun etc.

"There is no doubt that man saved our lives. He wasn't a Protestant either you know. I'll not name him. Of course he's dead years ago, but I'm still not going to name him."

Within a couple of months of all this, a plan was revealed to disarm the RUC, something Drew believes was entirely a political decision and one that left his men desperately exposed – or would have done had he not been willing to stand up to senior officers.

"The Bessbrook tender landed out; they used to bring stores and what-not out to us. I was chatting away to them and I asked 'what are you out for today'? They said 'we're out to collect your guns'.

I said 'you're friggin' joking; you're getting no guns here and you tell the County [Inspector] if he takes the guns out of this station, he may provide accommodation for me, my wife and family, and every man that's stationed here. By this time there was a Sergeant and 12. The County Inspector eventually came out to see me and he and I had it hot and heavy. I was at the stage where I didn't give a damn you know – silly buggers.

"Anyway, he was also adamant - again for political reasons - that we weren't building any sandbag emplacements. But there was a big pile of sandbags left over from the previous troubles that ended in '62. So I got the boy at Newtownhamilton who looked after maintenance to deliver me a load of sand and we built the sanger ourselves at the front door of the station. There was a fella with us, Bob, who had been a bricklayer by trade. And he built it. You've never seen as neat a sanger in your life.

"I never saw another officer after that; not a soul came near us. That was until Captain Orr, who at that time was a government minister, decided he would pay us a visit in Cross. And I thought 'the shit will really hit the fan now because the County Inspector will be with him and he'll see this sanger and go doolally. So Orr arrived up, saw the sanger and started immediately to praise it for how it was built. He was a former army man and he tried all the sightlines for shooting etc and said he had never seen such a well-built sanger. I could see the County Inspector's face and he was raging but he couldn't say a thing.

"So then he came back later on to argue about the guns. I said 'you can take the guns if you want but I'll turn the lock on the door and we'll all go in with you. So we came to an agreement that we could keep three Sterling submachine guns.

"They took my sidearm and everything so I said in that case I don't want to live here with my family, unable to defend them. He asked if I wanted a transfer and I said I did. I didn't really as I didn't want to abandon the boys in it." But Drew was transferred – to Portadown.

As he packed up in Crossmaglen, he was painfully aware of how the situation was changing and how it seemed there was little he or anyone else could do. A terrible monster had been given life. Forcing it back into its lair would take three decades and cost thousands of lives.

Soon, in Bessbrook, with a heavy heart, a police officer would add the first two names to the map...

The red Ford Cortina, stolen from outside a hotel in Newry, had sat just off the Lisseraw Road, around a mile from Crossmaglen, for two days. It was almost half eight on a light August evening, when two young constables, Sam Donaldson and Roy Millar, walked up to it. They were armed with nothing more deadly than a length of curtain wire. Easing the door-skin outwards, they pushed the wire down behind it and wriggled it until it caught the door's locking mechanism. A quick upwards tug and the lock popped. As they opened the door, the interior light came on. It sent a small charge along a hidden wire, detonating a bomb which killed the two young men, and ushered in a new era of shocking violence, violence that had previously been unimaginable, violence where the victims were more often than not, literally, blown to pieces.

The two constables were blown right over a hedge and into a field. Both were horribly injured but conscious. Roy had been courting a local girl, Ann Donaldson, and her brother was one of the first to arrive at the scene. A clearly shocked and confused Roy asked him: "Is Ann ok?"

Sgt McCrum, who had replaced Drew, was also on the scene quickly and Roy said: "God save me, I'm going to die. You're a good sergeant. I like you. See you in heaven."

Constable Roy Millar was killed when he and his colleague Sam Donaldson tripped a booby trap bomb in a stolen car they were examining.

Both men died early the next morning in Daisy Hill Hospital.........

Roy Millar smiles for the camera as he stands, hands crossed in front of him, warming himself by a cosy-looking fire in the married quarters in Crossmaglen. He's there visiting Drew and his family. It's 1969. In another shot, he has joined them for a day out during their holiday in a caravan at Cranfield.

Drew's wife handles the 50-year-old photos with delicacy and fondness, their value to her easy to see. Even after all these decades, to her and her family, Roy is not just a dot on the map; he is, and will forever be a handsome, fun-loving young man with a strong Ballymena accent and wicked sense of humour. After his first time on the beat, Drew had asked him how he'd got on with the locals. He smiled as he replied : "Great: they couldnae understand a wurd ah said and ah couldnae understand a wurd they said."

Many wreaths were sent to the funerals of the two constables from the people of Crossmaglen. In his book 'Bandit Country', Toby Harnden quotes an IRA volunteer named only as 'M'. He said: "I knew Constable Donaldson very well and Constable Miller boarded here in a local house. I was genuinely sorry for them when they were killed. There was no pleasure in that. They were victims of the British presence here. They were genuine victims of what had been wrong and continues to be wrong in the Six Counties. But in the atmosphere of the time down here killing them was an unpopular act."

* Surname withheld

** The B Men, or B Specials, were part of the Ulster Special Constabulary. They were unpaid part-timers. Composed almost entirely of Protestants, they were distrusted by the nationalist community.

*** Tynan is a small village in County Armagh.

**** A 6 km stretch of the Republic of Ireland's N53 is actually in Northern Ireland where, for historic reasons, it is known as Concession Road.

The Map

2

Ballgowns and Blood Trails

Fate: fat, n. Inevitable destiny or necessity: appointed lot.

Providence: prov i-dens, n. The foresight and benevolent care of God.

Chance: chans, n. That which falls out fortuitously, or without assignable cause

There's nothing exceptional about the blue Toyota Corolla parked on Newry's Merchants' Quay, nothing to make you look a second time. An anonymous family workhorse of a car, chosen for exactly that reason; its ability to merge into its surroundings.

But if you were to look, very closely, you might just notice that a neat, square hole has been cut out of the boot lid, just beside the number plate. A piece of card, exactly the same colour as the car, is glued over the hole.

Fate is shuffling its cards.......

Paul Slaine was working in the collator's office, sifting through intelligence documents. This wasn't his usual job – he was covering another officer's leave – but he enjoyed the work and seemed to have an aptitude for it.

He wasn't expecting to leave the station that day, at least not until a detective poked his head into the room. They needed a volunteer to help with a Crown Court case in Armagh.

"The defence had introduced alibi evidence around timings. The detective told me: 'We need to get someone to walk the route the guy claims to have taken. We'll time it and then you'll have to make a statement and go to Armagh to introduce the evidence in court.'

"I said that was grand. A couple of lads from the CID office drove me out and dropped me off. I walked the route, they timed it, and I came back into the station and wrote my statement."

Paul borrowed a jacket and tie from a colleague, drove to Armagh and gave his evidence. By this time, it was nearly six o'clock. He could have gone straight home from Armagh. He could have, but he didn't. He decided instead to return the jacket and tie and file the necessary paperwork. He didn't know it but his life was turning inexorably on these small decisions. He phoned his wife when he got back to Newry, telling her not to worry about dinner, that he would eat at the station before setting out for home.

But fate was already dealing the cards……

"There was only me and the staff in the canteen. They made me a bite to eat and I was just sitting down to it when my Sergeant came in. He was getting himself a cup of tea. I explained what I was doing there and he asked 'Could you stay on? There's a threat and we're short of people'. And I thought 'Well, I'm here, so I may as well stay'."

Later, much later, even years later, in the long, dark nights, when pain pushes away any hope of sleep, Paul will go over again and again in his head all the choices that he made that evening, playing out alternative scenarios, torturing himself with thoughts of 'What if' or 'If only……'.

He was teamed up with a sergeant called Mervyn, and a Constable called Colleen McMurray. Colleen was one of four daughters from a farming family. She grew up near the village of Sixmilecross in County Tyrone and had joined the police straight from school in 1976. The three set out on patrol.

The thing with fate, though, is that every move counts……

"Sometime around nine o'clock we all got called back to the station and we were told 'The threat has gone up again; there's to be no routine patrolling'.

"We were going to do security points at Downshire Road, which was the Mobile Support Unit (MSU) base, and round the station or whatever, but weren't to be out patrolling.

"We had no specifics on the threat. But I went to Newry in September '88 and from then until March '92, I was never at a briefing where the threat went down. It was always going up, up, up. What you've got to remember is that in '85 and '86 you'd had the mortar attack, you'd had Killeen, you'd had people killed in the square. I think in the space of 18 months you'd had something like 18 police officers killed. It was absolutely terrible. But from '86 through to '92, no police officer had been killed in Newry itself, but the threat was always going up - and the desire was there.

"So, we were back in the station, it was after nine o'clock. My wife, who's a nurse was going to work at 10, and at this stage we were being told we weren't going out although nobody knew what time we'd be getting away. So I took the final chance to ring her before she left for work and I told her 'there's something going on, we're all in the station'."

Sometime around 11 o'clock, they were given the green light to go back out and do security checks known as 'seals'. Now, though, there was only Paul and Colleen. Mervyn had gone home as his son was ill and had to be taken to hospital. Paul took over as driver. They were sent back out to clear routes that would shortly be used by fellow officers coming on night duty.

They set up a checkpoint at Downshire Road. "One of my lasting memories of that evening is how Colleen, who came from a farming background, had stopped a guy in a big Toyota Land Cruiser with a cattle trailer on behind and the two of them were having the best laugh. She was laughing, he was laughing; it was just one of those typical, lovely, warm moments you got with Colleen.

Back on Merchants' Quay, the blue Toyota sat in brooding silence…

"A call came over the radio. It was coming near finishing time, maybe 11:30. A woman had locked herself out of her car in Sugar Island in the centre of the town - could we go and help her out? So we just drove slowly back into the town. And when we were nearly there, probably passing Downshire Road, one of the other call signs came on to say 'we're already at that, we'll sort it out'.

"We drove past and we were actually tooting the horn and waving as if to say 'ha ha, we're getting away here and you're stuck'."

It was almost midnight and punters were spilling out of the local pubs and nightclubs. The straight route back to the station was via Monaghan Street but it was crammed with people most of whom had been drinking. To avoid any possible confrontation, Paul turned right on to Merchants' Quay.

And, finally, fate showed its hand…

In the boot of the Toyota was a Mk 12 mortar, lined up to fire through the square cut-out. On the other side of the canal, the IRA team stood up and triggered a handheld photographer's flash gun. This prompted a second flash from a 'slave' unit in the car and, in turn, fired the mortar with its improvised warhead containing 1-2lbs of Semtex, a Czech-made plastic explosive which had been shipped to the IRA in vast amounts by Libya's Colonel Gaddaffi. The Semtex had travelled thousands of miles to reach this particular place at this particular time. The warhead had to travel less than eight feet to find its target. It slammed into Paul and Colleen's car.

"I knew that something had happened. I can't remember hearing an explosion, but I knew something had happened and I was conscious of the car still moving. I thought I was trying to brake, but the car kept rolling and it rolled all the way along Merchants' Quay until it hit a parked car.

"I have a vague memory of somebody appearing at the door and then that was it. I just don't remember anything after that, until I started to come round which was in the Royal Victoria Hospital. I thought that it was maybe the next day but I now know I was out of it for a couple of weeks between morphine and being in an induced coma and all that sort of stuff. It wasn't until then that I saw my Sergeant and my Inspector standing with my wife at the foot of the bed telling me about Colleen. I had asked a number of times: 'Where is she, where is she?' They then broke the news to me but I was so heavily sedated I couldn't even cry. They were trying to tell me that I had lost my legs but I couldn't even compute that."

The car Paul had been driving

Overcome by her injuries, Colleen had died in hospital in the early hours of the following morning. She was 34. The sadness was palpable as her name was added to the map.

If fate had conspired against Paul this far, it was now the turn of providence - or chance. However you look at it; there is no doubt he owes his life to a string of incredible coincidences.

"There were two paramedics parked outside A&E at Daisy Hill. They had picked somebody up, a drunk or whatever, and had brought him up to Daisy Hill. They were in the ambulance tidying up, doing whatever paperwork they had to do and they heard the explosion.
"It was so loud, the guys in the station thought the station had been mortared. But these two paramedics thought 'that's in the town centre' and before they had even been dispatched, before they received any comms or anything, they were off, racing down Monaghan Street. They turned on to Merchants' Quay, into the one-way system, and came on the incident. I was in the road.

"They couldn't get Colleen out of the car. So the first ambulance that came I was literally on to the gurney and away which meant I was in hospital very quickly after the incident. By the time I'd got to Daisy Hill, there was obviously a wee bit of a delay – ten or fifteen minutes – but well within the 'golden hour' as they talk about. MSU (Mobile Support Unit) were doing security at the hospital. They had been dispatched because they knew we were being brought in. I talked to one of those guys recently and he said they were standing there and couldn't believe what they were seeing. He says he just couldn't believe that I would survive, seeing the state in which they brought me in."

A few miles away, meanwhile, scores of pagers and bleepers began to go off simultaneously. The Daisy Hill Hospital annual ball was taking place in the Marine Court Hotel in Warrenpoint.

"So that particular time on a Friday night normally you would have had maybe a junior house doctor and a few staff on duty or whatever. All these folk; anaesthetists, surgeons, everybody, they were all at this function in the Marine Court, ten or fifteen minutes away. By the time the two of us were in hospital there were two full surgical teams working on us."

Many of the medics worked throughout the night in bow ties, dinner suits and ballgowns but they just couldn't save Colleen. Paul, however, knows it is just one of a string of coincidences that saved his life. "I mean some of these people lived in parts of the Republic, they lived away in Lurgan or Armagh or wherever. If they had to be called in from home, I'd never have made it.

"Even at the scene I was fortunate. When the mortar hit the car door, it hit it roughly where the mirror would be. On the inside of the police car doors at that time they had like a metal plate, maybe 10mm thick. It was bolted in at a couple of points top and bottom. The plastic on the inside of the door was completely gone. The steel had a massive hole in it, but the plate itself was actually lying in the car so I think that's probably what took my legs off.

"The whole dashboard was missing from the car, the armoured glass was all fractured, all the panels round the car and the roof were ripped off. Because the driver's door was so badly damaged, obliterated really, they were able to get me out right away at the scene."

Paul's wife, a nurse, was at work. It was around midnight and all was quiet. The patients were in bed and she was just doing her rounds when she heard a car outside. She thought it was the night duty officer coming round to check all was ok. She walked down, looked out through the window and she saw Paul's Inspector walking up the steps. His Sergeant was waiting in the car.

"When she saw the Inspector's face, she ran, she ran down the ward because she thought I was dead.

"So it was both my sergeant and my inspector in the car with my wife. They said 'Look, we have to get you down to Newry' and she said 'I want you to tell me now; is he dead?' And my inspector answered: 'no, no he's not'. Truthfully, he didn't know at that time as there were no mobile comms."

They drove to Newry and stopped initially at the police station. This was to allow the inspector, who like everyone else who had seen the extent of Paul's injuries, feared the worst, to go inside and find out what the situation was before going to the hospital. Paul was clinging to life. So he came back out, got into the car again and drove up to A&E.

"My wife said whenever they got out at the main doors and walked through she just followed the massive trail of blood all the way to the theatre doors. She was stopped there and told she couldn't come in. She says there was blood everywhere."

Colleen survived until the early hours.

"The duty Inspector that night and his staff went out and picked up her mum and dad and they got them to Daisy Hill, I think, just about the time that she died. She had been married about 18 months and her husband was also a police officer and some of the guys out of our section had gone to their home, picked him up and brought him down.

"In the middle of all this, the crowd that had been around the Town Hall – they rioted at the scene. There was a whole melee. My wife was put into a side room and she could see all these people coming in saying they were injured. Unbeknownst to her, these were the ones who had been rioting at the scene. But the police had fired baton rounds and a number of these individuals had been hit so they were in A&E and I think at some point there was a realisation 'We've got all his colleagues in here, we've got an MSU in here and we're now bringing in individuals who were possibly involved in some way' so I think things were a bit tense in the hospital to put it mildly. Even my wife says if she had known at the time who they were she wouldn't have been responsible for what she would have done. So that's obviously why they kept her offside."

For Paul, a long, painful period that would demand from him every ounce of his courage and resilience was just beginning, but there was one key duty to be performed first. Just before the mortar hit, he had seen two men, who he recognised as IRA members, watching him from the street and he was determined to get that information out.

"I had a tracheostomy tube inserted and was wearing an oxygen mask so I couldn't really speak. But I had been trying to ask where I was and one of the nurses had bent down and explained 'You're in the Royal Victoria Hospital'. And apparently I got really agitated, you know thrashing about on the bed and whatnot. And she said 'You're okay, you're okay, there are policemen outside the door'."

A number of people, over the years, had been attacked in the Royal by the IRA whose West Belfast heartland was within easy striking distance.

"Anything I'd ever heard about the Royal was people getting attacked and murdered you know. So I'm in bed, really agitated and she's saying 'It's okay there are police outside the door'. And apparently then I kind of calmed down. But at some stage, when I had come off the drugs and was starting to come round, I was trying to talk.

"I couldn't speak and my wife said 'we think he's trying to tell us something'. I was asking, as best I could, for a 'pen'. They kept thinking I was saying 'pain' and giving me more morphine and woosh I would be out again. And this went on for a number of days.

"At one point, they had come in with a pen and clipboard and I had tried so hard to write that I burst stitches in my arm and had to be taken back to theatre. But I came round at one stage and my wife was standing beside the bed and she said 'Paul, are you trying to tell us something?' And I nodded and she said 'Well, what is it?' And this time I used my hands to make a very basic alphabet and I spelled out the names of the two individuals who I had seen at the time of the explosion. From the moment I had come round, I had been thinking those two were on the street near where this happened and they were two known players. And I wanted to get the names out. So she said 'I'll go and get your Inspector' and he appeared in the ward and asked what I was trying to tell them. I spelled out the names of these two individuals again. I'll not name them here, but he said 'Are you saying that you saw So-and-so and So-and-so there that night? And then he said 'Right, I'm away to tell CID' and at that point I kind of relaxed because I had got that off my chest.

"Of all the people I could have named, of all the people I could have said that I had seen – you know people were trying to say 'Maybe you imagined it, maybe it's the morphine' and stuff like that - but whenever you look back on it, as my wife says, you're struck by the amount of time and effort it took me just to get those two names to them. They were never confirmed as having taken part but there was an event on that night in the Town Hall which was used as a cover for this incident and for people being in the area. And, at the end of the day, I suspect that some individuals would have probably been doing like an outer perimeter, keeping an eye on who was about and what was about and whatever.

"At every point, when you are alone in hospital, things go around in your head. People have kind of lost sight of this these days; if you talk to people nowadays, they can't really get their head around it, but back then families couldn't go straight to the Royal because of the threat so they had to go to Grosvenor Road police station and get into one of the police Land Rovers which was then escorted by the military to the hospital. The military then did foot patrols around the grounds while the relatives were in visiting you.

"Accidentally, one of the police officers happened to mention one day about the big threat of a Mk 12 mortar attack on the Westlink. So maybe at one o'clock I'd be sitting upright in the bed. Visiting time was at two. For that hour I would be hyper-vigilant, waiting to hear a bang, an explosion or whatever. And then, whenever my wife and kids would come in, I would sigh and think 'Thank God'. Then when they would leave I would spend an hour listening for a bang again. Eventually I told the nurse you have to get me moved. I said I can't think, I'm just completely stressed here because I'm worried about something happening to my wife and kids and she said 'Leave it with me and I'll see what I can do'. So they got me transferred to the Ulster Hospital and it was only when I was sent there that I was able to start to settle a wee bit and think about trying to get better. I had been obsessed. Literally, just behind my head in the Royal, there was a door into a wee room and there were two police officers in there 24-7 and one of the nights the door knocked. This guy stepped in and he says 'Paul, I hope you don't mind, we have to close the door, there's a threat on'. And he went over to the door which was out onto the corridor or whatever and closed it and behind the door was a bullet-proof panel. The guy explained that if anybody wanted in, nurses or whoever, they would come to their door where they would check them then let them through. And I'm in hospital thinking 'I'm like a sitting duck here in this ward' and to try to explain to people nowadays that those were the circumstances; you know people look at you and say 'no there's no way'."

Learning to cope with such serious injuries, has been difficult for Paul's entire family.

"It's been a massive challenge. I suppose the saving grace has been my wife's background as a mental health nurse. We just chatted all the time. Some very frank conversations; I think at one stage I sort of tried to convince her to just leave, take the kids, move on. When this happened, my three children were all under 10. My youngest was just a baby of 10 months.

"Again, as time went on and you started chatting to them, as they got older, all the issues they were having became clear, like serious nightmares. Children pick up on snippets of conversation. They hear things like about me being guarded in hospital and stuff like that and they would wake up in the middle of the night shouting 'Are they going to come and kill daddy?'

"One of our daughters had written on an early Christmas list that she wanted new legs for daddy. My son has really suffered. He was only ten months at that time. He is thirty one now. But he was around my wife all the time then and the stress that she was under at home and the stress of having to come up and down to the hospital. And we ended up having to move house. Everything that was associated with that I think it has left a permanent mark on him in particular."

Paul returned to work in November 1993, a decision that was the subject of much stress in the family home.

"There were days where I was literally struggling for five minutes to lift the wheelchair out of the car to get out of the car and into work. But I didn't take a day's sick from then until I retired in 2021. I refused to buckle. I wanted to prove, not just to the police but to myself that what happened in Newry was not going to define me. I went in and did my best to be the best. I had a fulfilling career, thoroughly enjoyed it and I hope I made at least a bit of a difference. You can't explain it; the camaraderie, the sense of pride, you were conscious of whose shoulders you were standing on. When you passed the memorial, you kind of …… well, I don't know it's hard to explain but you were very aware of how those people had handed on the baton and it was you who had the job of carrying it now."

On Wednesday, April 12, 2000, Paul was chosen to receive the George Cross from the late Queen Elizabeth on behalf of the RUC in a ceremony at Hillsborough Castle. It was in recognition of the bravery of the force during the thirty years of the troubles. Queen Elizabeth

The late Queen Elizabeth II presents the George Cross to Paul Slaine. He received it on behalf of the RUC

paid tribute to the "terrible price" paid by the RUC as well as its courage and sense of duty.

"It wasn't until I got there that day, uniform on, the crowds, that it really hit about the sense of occasion and what was actually happening. There were widows there, there were children, injured police officers and you realise that this is a massive occasion, this was history being made. It was a really sombre occasion. A lot of people have asked me 'what did you actually say'. I don't really remember, but I do remember how, when she was handing the cushion to me, she had tears in her eyes and when I took the cushion I thought 'If a single tear runs down her face, I'll fold up into the middle of this wheelchair and go to pieces with all the media and everybody watching'. People sometimes say the George Cross was a sop to the RUC, an afterthought to soften the blow when all the things were being done to it. But that is one of the most expensive medals in the history of this country when you think of the blood that was spilled and lives that were lost.

"I've probably never dealt properly with Colleen's death, not being able to get to the funeral and that type of thing. Every year on Remembrance Sunday since then a number of us have gone down to the service in the wee church in Sixmilecross and one of the things that I reflect on is that there were six women police officers killed in the troubles. Four of those were killed in Newry and two of them are buried about 10 feet apart in this wee graveyard in Sixmilecross. Ivy Kelly, who was killed in the mortar attack, is buried in the same graveyard. So we go down every year, put flowers in the graveyard and go to the service. Colleen's mum and dad are dead now but we used to go back to the family home and spend a bit of time with them and chat with them. It was an important thing that I know we have never forgotten and will never forget."

The Map

3

Rubber Bounces Back

The man sitting across the table from me is not an urban myth. He really exists. This, let me tell you, is a surprise to me. What happened to him seemed the stuff of legend when I was younger; almost beyond belief. Yet, here he is, sitting opposite me in a hotel. His name is John Montgomery but he is pretty much universally known as 'Rubber'. This is his story…

"Somebody's hammering on the car; hammering on the floor of it. Who is it? We're upside down. Have they come to finish us off? 'Errol. Errol! F**k me Errol, we've been blown up'. My eyes, ears, mouth and nose are full of glass and dust. There's bleeding. I know there's bleeding. I need to get a dressing on Errol's wound. My f****ng rifle has snapped in two. I've got my revolver but I'm thinking 'can I use it?' Is the floor of this car armoured? I can hear someone outside shouting: 'Burn the bastards'."

Five minutes earlier…

It is Sunday, September 21, 1986. Call sign Hotel Bravo Seven Zero, a red armoured 1600 Austin Maestro, is snaking its way along the A25 just outside the village of Camlough. It's the car's first outing. It has only 96 miles on the clock and is filled 'to the neck' with petrol. Rubber is observer. He's in the passenger seat and feeling a little delicate after a night out. He's only 22 but looks even younger. His more experienced colleague, Errol, is driving.

"It was foggy," recalls Rubber "and the fog always sat, at certain times of year, on Camlough mountain."

Perhaps it was that fog that had allowed the bombers to go about their business unseen, perhaps they had worked out a 'blind spot', out of sight of the army observation post that clung to the mountain high above the Camlough Road

Whatever the case, they had somehow managed to dig in an 800lbs landmine and run a command wire all the way to the Church Rock Road and a hidden location that afforded them a view of all traffic on the road below – including Hotel Bravo Seven Zero.

"Me and Errol tended to go places back then that maybe we shouldn't have gone to all the time," says Rubber.

"We did the warrants from Bessbrook so we would have driven around the area at different times of day. I suppose we did try to 'risk assess' it as such – if that's a phrase you want to use.

"The station sergeant loved us because we were the only people who would do the warrants in Silverbridge and places like that."

Were they where at this point was actually considered, relatively, safe. "You weren't allowed to go beyond Camlough onto the Sturgeon or Crossmaglen roads or out towards Belleeks because there had been landmines there before. But this part of the road was considered safe because it was still sort of built up."

What happened next is still hard to explain, all these decades later. Was it the hyper-vigilance that came with being a police officer in this dangerous place, was it subconsciously registered clues that said 'something's not right' or was it, as Rubber himself puts it, a sixth sense?

"So we're driving down the road, just past Gregory's garage, and I says to Errol 'I f****ng hate this road' and he says 'Rubber; I f****ng hate it too' and he puts the foot down.

"And it's a weird thing, even today. I glanced up and there was a speed limit sign, you know when you're leaving the 30s, and I just glanced at it and said to myself, or I could have said it out loud, 'Something's going to happen and it's going to happen…. now'! And that is just exactly when it did happen. It was like some sort of sixth sense. I just glanced up at the sign and then it all went dark and there was just this low thud.

"People ask me what it was like and I always say you know those shots you see, that footage of hurricanes in the Caribbean where the trees are all bent over by the force of the hurricane? Well there are hawthorn hedges on either side of the Camlough Road there and for the first split-second that's what it was like before everything went dark."

That unexplained decision, to suddenly accelerate the car, almost certainly saved the lives of both men.

At the other end of the command wire, the would-be killers, caught by surprise, pushed the button just a split-second too late. The rear quarter panel of the armoured car took the brunt of the explosion.

It was 4:38 PM.

"So I remember looking across at Errol, because obviously the windscreen had shattered and all that type of stuff, and he's trying desperately to steer the car but the car, unbeknownst to us, had lifted into the air and he's still trying to steer it.

"This is all in the course of half a second; I'm thinking F**k, we've been blown up and we've sort of survived it. Now, will we survive the crash? Because if you crash in an armoured car, I know how dangerous that is. I was as scared of the crash as the bomb.

"So then the car obviously bounced and I remember it rolling and lucky enough it only rolled a couple of times before landing in the field. But then it landed in a shuck upside down and it began to fill with water and I was thinking 'F**k me, we've survived the bomb, we've survived the crash and now we're going to f****ng drown'.

"I just turned round to Errol and said 'F**k me Errol, we've been blown up' and there was no answer from him.

"We're upside down in the car. Errol's not in good shape; he's wearing body armour and I'm not and his thighs are pushing the body armour against his neck. So not only is he unconscious trying to come round from the head injury and with a big lump of armoured door against his arm so he can't feel it, but his body armour is actually choking him. If I had been unconscious, he would have survived all that had happened - only to die from choking on the body armour."

It was about now that Rubber began to consider the possibility that the team who had detonated the bomb could be making their way across the fields to finish him off.

"I had a quick look round the car before I even looked at Errol to see if the doors moved or if there would be any way out of it.

"I had glass in my eyes and my ears and my mouth. I knew there was bleeding. I could see, as the dust lifted, that Errol was bleeding. He then began to come round and he thought he had lost his arm because of this big lump of a door lying on him.

"I pulled him back the right way around and put a field dressing on his head where he had quite a bad injury."

Rubber began to search for his Ruger rifle, only to find it had been broken into two pieces. A wooden fencepost that had penetrated his seat also bore witness to the incredible force of the explosion and crash.

"Obviously, when we were tumbling round, I wasn't sitting straight and the fence post came through right where I would have been sitting. Somebody was looking out for me, the great architect of the universe was looking after me that day.

"Then we began to hear somebody hammering on the outside of the car and they're shouting: 'Is anybody alive in there?

"So I'm in two minds you know. I'm thinking 'Is it the Provos; are they going to come down?' Because obviously I had worked out there had been a command wire so that meant they were watching and they weren't far away. Will they walk down the field and finish us off?

"The Ruger rifle, like I said, has broken in two. So I've got my revolver out and I'm looking up at the bottom of the car and I'm thinking 'In an armoured car, is the bottom armoured? Because we've survived all this and, you know, if I fire a couple of shots off, will they ricochet around inside? These are the things going through your head."

More people began to arrive. Many of them drunk. "Now what the media said later was that local people had arrived to help out, but there were boys with a load of beer taken who wanted to set fire to the car. They were shouting 'Burn the bastards' and that sort of stuff you know.

"Then I heard the chopper and I'm thinking 'Surely the chopper won't let anything happen'. But then I remembered another incident, outside Cullyhana, where the chopper had the drop on the boys and didn't take the opportunity and I'm starting to think 'F**k, maybe they won't [save us]'. Then I heard the sirens and I thought 'We're going to be all right'."

In fact, the hammering on the car was the driver of another vehicle trying to help. The man, from the County Armagh village of Killylea, had been driving behind the police car when it was attacked. Rubber has never heard the man's name nor had a chance to thank him but he's very clear in his memory that people like him, who wanted to help, were in the minority that day.

"The police press office obviously saw an opportunity to say that local people had come out and risked their own lives to help. It never happened like that.

"Anyway, some people pushed the car back over which meant we were upside down again and Erroll lost his field dressing and started to bleed again. So eventually I ripped the door open and I remember seeing Nigel, an ex-Para who was in my section in Bessbrook, and he's holding the crowd back with his rifle and he keeps glancing round at the door of the car because I think he's just expecting it to be mush you know.

"Just when we're talking about fate and that, I'll tell you something about Nigel. He had been in the Paras but wanted to join the police and he was away doing his interview for the police on the day all his mates were killed at Narrow Water.

"Anyway, he's looking round really concerned thinking 'F**k me, it's Rubber and Errol', you know all that sort of stuff. And then I popped my head out and it was just relief really from everybody. The ambulance man and the Fire Brigade they wanted to get me out and I said 'No, get Errol out because he's injured'. So we pulled him across and I wanted to deal with him, to put the field dressing back on again. It was covered in dirt by this stage, but they couldn't sort of placate me. Of course your heart rate, you know, the adrenaline is really going. The ambulance man says, 'I'll do that young fella' and he put a brand-new dressing on him and I said 'right, I have to see the hole'."

It was what happened next that gave this event almost mythical status. Rubber, blood flowing from shrapnel wounds, jumped down into the vast crater, lay on his front in the rapidly-filling puddle and began to push out regulation press-ups and 'burpees'

"I must have looked like a ghost, covered in dust and glass and all this sort of stuff.

"And people were staring at me and I said: 'Well, they're not going to see me feeling sorry for myself, crying or any of that so that's when I did the press ups and burpees -just to show I was still alive you know."

John (Rubber) Montgomery in an image captured moments after the landmine attack that almost killed him.

Rubber and Errol were sent to the police rehabilitation centre in Harrogate.

"Errol was older than me and I think it took him a bit of time to get over it.

"Anyway at Harrogate loads of people recognised me and came up to talk to me. It was a rare piece of good news. At that time, there was no good news coming out of Newry subdivision and this was a really good bit of news - that somebody, somehow, had survived a bomb."
Surely, nobody would ever come as close to being a dot on the map but live to tell the tale.

Rubber knew he and Errol had been incredibly lucky that day. But as the IRA famously warned after the Brighton hotel bombing "Today, we were unlucky, but remember we have only to be lucky once. You have to be lucky always."

And they were lucky in South Armagh – many times. This book features Rubber's story to underline the fact that policing DID still go on in the area and that not every murder bid succeeded. But, 18 months earlier, policing in the area had been rocked to its foundations by the single biggest loss of life suffered by the RUC during the Troubles… the Newry mortar attack.

The Map

4

Mortars

"I've been to so many houses to break the news of the death of their loved one..."

Blue flash after blue flash lights the darkening winter sky. Terrifying explosions.

"And they always ask the same question…"

In the canteen, officers yell split-second warnings. But which way to run?

"Did they suffer?"

Too late. Dust, noise, blackness, screaming.

"If I can tell them their loved one didn't suffer, it's the only thing, right there and then, that seems to bring some relief."

On the map, the town (now city) of Newry has a rectangle drawn around it in pen. A line runs from this box to a large space near the margin and here are written fifty one names. Among them are nine who all died on the same day - February 28, 1985:

They were Alexander Donaldson, Geoffrey Campbell, John Dowd, Denis Price, Rosemary McGookin, Sean McHenry, David Topping, Paul McFerran, and Ivy Kelly

They were all police officers and they were all killed when one of nine mortars fired by the IRA landed directly on the canteen in the police station at Corry Square.

All that was left of the canteen at Corry Square police station in Newry after it suffered a direct hit from an IRA mortar in February 1985. Nine police officers died in the attack.

The home-made mortars, known as Mark 10s were nasty, crude weapons designed with one thing in mind: to cause as much death and suffering as they possibly could. The tubes were made from modified Oxyacetylene bottles, while the projectiles were CO2 canisters - commonly used in the bar trade - which the IRA bomb-makers filled with a homemade explosive, a mixture of ammonium nitrate and nitro-benzine, known as ANNIE. The tubes were then welded on to a metal frame which was secured to the floor of a vehicle.

In this case, it was a Ford D-series flatbed lorry, the sort you would usually associate with things like coal rounds or timber deliveries. It had been hijacked earlier in Crossmaglen. The bombers drove into Monaghan Street in Newry, parking about sixty yards from the police station. The firing mechanism was on a timer so, by the time the first mortar left its tube, the killers had already made good their escape. As they fled, they left behind almost unimaginable horror and grief.

The mortars were notoriously inaccurate and more landed outside the police station walls than inside. But the one direct 'hit' caused the RUC's biggest ever loss of life in a single incident.

As the divisional commander, Bill Stewart, turned the key in his front door, he could hear the phone in the hall already ringing. "No mobiles in those days."

As he picked up, he immediately recognised the voice. It was John, a communications officer.

Bill recalls how John told him: "The place is wrecked. There's been a bomb, a mortar bomb."

"I asked him if anybody was injured and he said: 'Oh sir, there's bodies all over the yard!" I'll never forget how he said it - 'bodies all over the yard'."

Bill jumped into his car, turned around and drove back to Newry, back to the scene of carnage and to day after day of visiting bereaved families, struggling to tell them something, anything, that could make sense out of all this shock and pain.

The most high-ranking officer who died at Newry that day was Alex Donaldson, a brother of Sam Donaldson who was killed in Crossmaglen all those years earlier.

Bill recalls: "The last house we went to was Donaldsons'. I can remember going into the house and the three children were sitting in their dressing gowns on the settee, his wife was sitting there also. At that time I had two children about the same age and for the first time I had to walk out the door and compose myself.

"It was a house just like mine would have been with those children sitting ready for bed with their wee teddies or whatever. I get emotional even now thinking about it. Those are the things that stick in your head. I never could say that I didn't take very personally every death that happened in the area."

This is a man of courage and resolve who has been tested many times and proved his mettle many times. But there are tears in his eyes and just a hint of a tremble in his voice.

"Even yet, even yet, I get emotional about those things. You never really get used to it. You handle it but when you go home and put your head on the pillow…"

Bill knows he was lucky to escape with his own life that evening. He and a colleague had been at a meeting earlier that day. They had travelled in his car and he recalls how, at one point, they had spotted a young lad "running like a whippet" along the footpath with several uniformed officers struggling to keep with him. The two men in the car couldn't help but smile thinking how they might tease the chasers when they saw them later. This was normal policing, this was camaraderie – this was all about to change. The late Queen Elizabeth II famously said that grief was the price we paid for love. Camaraderie of the sort that tied police officers together at this time came at a similar high cost. I have interviewed or just chatted with many, many police officers from the 'Troubles' era. Not one would want to go back there, but just about all of them miss the unique bond forged and fastened by constant danger, by working as a team, a tight team, making the difference between life and death.

After their meeting, Bill and his colleague stopped outside the station and the colleague invited him in for a cup of tea. But Bill had another meeting to attend later. He said goodbye and drove on.

As he walked among the bodies later that evening, he knew there would be no banter about the chasing cops they'd seen earlier. Some of them, he thought, could even be among the dead. It would be a long time before smiles and laughter returned to Corry Square station.

At the other end of the rank structure from Bill, was a young constable I'm calling Jack - although that's not his real name. He and his colleagues had been out on the ground when the mortars struck. They made their way back to the station and were among the first people to be confronted by the unfolding horror. "It was carnage; that's the only word for it, carnage. There really did seem to be bodies everywhere."

But through the blackness, the chaos and the confusion shone two steady guiding lights in the form of duty and training. Quickly, Jack and his colleagues found themselves cordoning off the surrounding streets; preserving possible crime scenes and keeping routes free for ambulances. And it was those emergency vehicles, struggling in vain to help, that left Jack with one of his defining memories of that night.

An IRA unit just after test-firing a so-called 'Barrack-buster' homemade mortar similar to the one that hit the canteen in Corry Square police station with such devastating results.

"I can remember the fleet of ambulances coming past and people, mainly women, clapping and cheering - not in support you understand but in celebration, celebration of the fact that the station had been hit and delight in the unfolding scale of the loss of life."

At this time, Jack was considered a senior man. He was 22 years old. But these things, I guess, are relative. As Jack's sergeant ran his eye over the parade room at the nearby Downshire Road Station, he was met with anxious gazes from probationers as young as 18 or 19, little more than children who, confused and frightened, were looking to him for answers.

"I remember that big sergeant - his name was Gary - grabbed me and another more experienced constable and told us to go round all those who were gathering in the parade room, get their locker numbers and keys and a list of what they needed – mostly uniforms, body armour, that type of thing. We were then to go and get it for them."

Jack and his colleague were soon to discover just why they'd been given this order. To get to the lockers, they had to walk through a temporary morgue which had been set up in the back yard at Corry Square.

"He obviously didn't want the young probationers going in and seeing what was going on. So we went for the first run. There were eight of the nine bodies laid out on this green tarpaulin and it was just an absolute mess. They were recognisable as human torsos but you couldn't have identified anybody.

"I remember walking past one of the Scenes of Crime Officers (SOCOs) and he said 'listen guys, is there anything you can help us with here? I looked and thought 'I'm the clever boy here, you know, I'm suddenly a forensic scientist'. On one of the torsos there was the collar of a uniform with the harp and crown. It was actually within the torso but you could still see it, and I said: 'yes, that's a uniformed officer.' The SOCO asked me what had made me say that and I said 'the collar badge, a harp and crown'. He just looked at me and said: 'Don't be so presumptuous.' And we walked on.

"I went on down towards the locker rooms and the first one I went into happened to be the one that contained my locker. And I saw another SOCO working at the locker next to mine. He had a red bottle of Old Spice talc in his left hand and he was just steadily running a brush up and down it dusting it for fingerprints."

The locker belonged to one of the dead, and they were trying to get prints off his bottle of Old Spice as part of the effort to identify his body.

"And I think that was the moment it all came home to me, the reality of it. It wasn't the whole crime scene, the devastation or seeing the bodies. It wasn't any of that; it was my colleague's Old Spice talc being fingerprinted. It brought a moment of realisation. And when people mention the mortar attack, thirty, I suppose nearly forty, years on my mind goes to that bottle of Old Spice talc. For years and years and years, I couldn't walk into a chemist shop; just the smell of a chemist shop was too much for me."

After four or five runs in a Land Rover, Jack and his colleague had kitted out everybody in the parade room with at least the minimum they needed to let them get started.

That task complete, he was teamed up with three other officers for mobile patrol duties; Gary, the sergeant, and two constables who would themselves be killed just a few weeks later; Tracy Doak and Ronnie Baird. The four were expected, somehow, despite all they seen that night, to perform normal policing duties.

"I don't remember what we did but it would have been accidents, assaults, whatever; just normal policing work. What I do remember - again - is going to places and being jeered at. I remember driving through the town and there were boys coming out of bars celebrating. There was a sense of elation among some people. This was a big event and we had been beaten. We were taking a lot of abuse and a lot of stick."

The investigation into the mortar attack had already begun and at one point, they were deployed in support of a team sent to arrest the prominent Newry republican Eamon Collins at his home in Barcroft Park. At this time, he was a leading light in the IRA but he would go on to be a reviled figure in the republican movement when he became an informer and one of its fiercest critics. He was eventually beaten to death by unknown assailants as he walked near his home in Newry in 1999.

In the early hours of Friday morning, Jack and his colleagues returned to the station.

"We drove into the yard about three o'clock in the morning. Tracy was driving and she drove over something and damaged the sump of the car. 'What'll we do? What'll we do?' she was saying. And we told her; 'Just park it up. Have you seen the state of the place? Who's going to say anything about a bit of damage to the sump of an armoured Cortina. Now bear in mind we are in the inquiry office. Out that door is the temporary morgue for the eight bodies and we are in having our cup of tea. And Tracy is upset about this damage to the car saying 'I'm in trouble, I'm in trouble'. And then she got quite upset about Rosie McGookin. Tracy was getting married in the September and I think she was getting Rosie's wedding dress after it had been altered for her. And the big station sergeant heard this conversation as he walked in and took the duty sheet off the wall and set it on the front desk. I can remember him starting to cross out the names from D section. He crossed six names off that section and began to write in six new names provided by headquarters because, even at three o'clock in the morning, the system had swung into action. The people had to be replaced. The show had to go on. But these were lives that were being crossed out. Six guys out of a section. In those days in Newry there were maybe 18 in a section so there was a third of them gone.

"And it was true that you spent more time with your colleagues than you did with your family. They were your family. So I can remember him doing this and watching him out of the corner of my eye, watching the six new names going up in ballpoint ink. But on the side of all this, Tracy is having this conversation with somebody about her wedding dress. And the sergeant - he was a big strong character - turned round to Tracy and said: 'is that all you're f*****g worried about?' Tragically, six or seven weeks later, Tracy wasn't needing a wedding dress as she was killed at Killeen.

"And now I know that Tracy, twenty years of age or whatever she was, was just trying to cope that night. What had happened was just too much to take in so, as a form of self preservation, a kind of denial, I suppose, the brain settles on some irrelevant little things and that's what you focus on: the damaged sump or the wedding dress, but not those eight horribly mutilated bodies of our friends and colleagues lying only feet away. That's just so far beyond what your brain can process."

It's almost forty years since the mortar attack; four decades in which our understanding and treatment of the effects of trauma has been entirely transformed, four decades in which many people, left untreated and alone at the time, have lived with the debilitating reality of Post-Traumatic Stress Disorder.

"For those of us who survived that night, there was a feeling that we were somehow invincible. You could have gone and stood up at Killeen (border crossing point) with a beacon on your head and nothing was going to happen to you. Because the bad thing had happened, it had happened. There is nothing more they can do to us – we're safe now. There is a thing called survivors' guilt but there is also survivors' elation where you dust yourself down and just think 'it wasn't me'. You had a feeling almost like immortality, like what are they going to do now? They're going to leave us alone. They've hit us and now they'll leave us alone."

That feeling, of course, is an imposter every bit as much as the guilt and all the other feelings and emotions that swirl around in the aftermath of events like this with which we, as humans, are simply not designed to cope. Eventually, those emotions land on somebody and just like the physical dust and rubble that preceded them, the damage caused can be catastrophic.

Nine funerals followed over the coming days but Jack says nothing shook the resolve of those left behind for whom this was more than just a job.

"I can't remember ever wanting to leave Newry. I never thought 'I need to get out of here or it's my time for a transfer'. I always thought morale was okay. You wanted to come back in to get the job done. You almost had to be forced to take leave and when you did it was easy to find yourself sitting thinking 'I wonder what the lads are up to now'. You missed being there, missed being out with them. I can't say that morale got low at that stage; I can't say that. We just got on and did the job…."

The Map

5

Sniper

As it lifts off from Crossmaglen, the Lynx helicopter draws barely a glance from the locals. It's such a common occurrence that even the distinctive loud scream of its twin engines goes virtually unnoticed by the people going about their business below.

The low winter sunshine glints momentarily off its blades as it rolls slightly then disappears off towards Golf One Zero.

One of a network of ten watchtowers built by the army in the 1980s, Golf One Zero overlooks the village of Cullaville, the most southerly settlement in County Armagh straddling, as it does, the border with the Irish Republic.

Paul Young closes his eyes and briefly leans his head back against the straps and padding that line the inside of the Lynx. The former soldier, now a police officer, is mentally running through the items in his rucksack, checking them against the tasks for the carefully-planned patrol ahead.

It's a bright February day. The landscape below is undeniably beautiful, flooded now in milky sunlight that whispers of Spring. Just ahead, Lough Ross shimmers like polished silver, while behind nestles the Ring of Gullion, it's mysterious low rugged hills, draped in myth and legend.

In a matter of minutes, Paul and his colleagues are out of the helicopter and watching it fly back towards Crossmaglen. He glances at his team – a tight team, a capable team; made up of men specially chosen for this most dangerous of postings. He doesn't know it yet, but shortly he will be back on that helicopter, accompanying the dead body of one of those men who gather round him now in the shadow of Golf One Zero…

The teenage Derrick Paul Young made a little bit of military history from the moment he joined the army in 1968. He was the very last Royal Dragoon before that historic cavalry regiment, formed in the 1660s, was amalgamated with the Royal Horse Guards to form the Blues and Royals.

And it was with the Blues and Royals that Paul found himself in the grim surroundings of the Belfast of 1971.

"It was all a bit of a shock. Such was my naïveté, I thought the island of Ireland was still part of the United Kingdom and it was a sharp wake-up call to find out it was only Northern Ireland. My enduring memory of that winter is that it was a dark, dirty, cold monochrome place. I mean, there was colour but when you look back at it in your mind, it's monochrome."

To the exhausted young Troopers, it seemed like the riots would never stop. Every return to base meant repainting the vehicles that were constantly targeted with paint, blast and acid bombs. Sleep was hard to come by.

For Paul, it was a steep learning curve. The idea that this troubled place would be where he would eventually settle would have seemed laughable to the young soldier. But it was after a military career that took him all over the world, and back to Northern Ireland enough times to grow to care deeply about the place, he decided to join the RUC. He would eventually settle down with Heather, a County Down woman he describes simply as 'the love of my life'. Sadly, she was to die while still a young woman. Paul is a tough character, held in high regard by his 'brothers in arms', but the pain of that period in his life is impossible to hide – even for him.

Before all that, however, there was Crossmaglen.

After the Lynx left, Paul's primary patrol began to walk from Golf One Zero. Military satellite patrols offered further protection. In South Armagh at this time, extraordinary measures were required to provide ordinary policing.

The police and the military would plan patrol cycles in two-week blocks, deciding on priorities and tracing out routes the night before. "Who did we have to arrest? What summonses had to be served? What witnesses had to be interviewed after road traffic accidents? It was ordinary policing, just ordinary policing. The rest was just about trying to keep us alive."

On this particular day, Paul's colleague, John Reid, wanted to visit a family called White. Their daughter had been seriously injured in a road traffic accident and he wanted to check on her. John had only ten days left in

Soldiers had to accompany police officers much of the time in South Armagh with even the simplest policing task, such as serving a summons, requiring a great deal of planning and support.

Crossmaglen. He had been there for a long time and had just recently asked for, and got, a transfer to Armagh.

Part of the frustration of this type of policing was that you could never ring ahead; never make an arrangement to see people at a particular place and time. When they called at the White home, Paul recalls, nobody was there.

"I remember we sat having a cup of tea from a flask and just enjoying the beautiful day which was unusual. We had our satellite patrols around us doing what they did and we said 'right let's head back towards base'."

But something wasn't quite right. The soldiers in Golf One Zero had noticed a vehicle acting suspiciously on a road that overlooked Paul's patrol, and spotted a man walking across a field with his hood up despite the nice weather.

"They were too far away for any of the satellite patrols to pick them up and stop them. So we were aware of this and as we walked down the road towards Crossmaglen we had to make a decision about what to do."

In August 1992, Private Paul Turner, a soldier in the Light Infantry, was killed by a single shot as he stood in the main square in Crossmaglen. His death was the first in a series of such killings that were attributed to the South Armagh sniper. The "sniper", as initially portrayed though, was a myth. The myth suggested there was one

The infamous 'Sniper at Work' sign which helped create the inaccurate mythology around what were actually two teams of IRA gunmen.

man, possibly trained by a retired military expert, armed with a specialist US-made Barrett Light 50 rifle, who never missed.

The reality was very different. There was no single sniper but at least two teams of up to 20 people. While a Barrett rifle was used at times, it was only one of a range of weapons employed by the IRA. The skill level of the shooters was also far from military standard. Most shots were taken from less than 300 metres, even though the weapons had an effective range of up to 1,000 metres, and they missed more targets than they hit.

Nonetheless, the myth of the lone sharpshooter gained ground, assisted by the infamous 'sniper at work' sign which was erected in Crossmaglen and became an iconic image for the IRA in South Armagh and its supporters. The "sniper" was a useful propaganda and fundraising tool. For the police and soldiers on the ground, however, the results of these attacks were all too clear.

By the time the IRA teams were broken up and partially captured, ten security force members had lost their lives to a sniper attack; ten more dots on the map. The IRA viewed the operation as a success, having made life even more difficult for the police and army in the area. It made the security forces ever more dependent on helicopter transport and ceded some element of control of the ground to the IRA. In April, 1997, one of the two teams was captured by an SAS unit working with the RUC's Special Branch. Four men - Micheal Caraher, Bernard McGinn, James McArdle and Martin Mines - were arrested and eventually jailed. They served 18 months before they were released on licence under the terms of the Good Friday Agreement. A Barrett sniper rifle was seized. The second team was never caught and, in 2001 when the IRA began the process, as another part of the Good Friday Agreement, of putting its weapons "completely and verifiably beyond use", it was believed that it still had two Barrett rifles in its arsenal.

Paul's patrol decided to wait for the satellite teams to catch up. "That's what we did before making a decision about our next move." A car came along the road from the south. "I was down in the ditch. So was John, but for some reason or another he decided to get up and do a stop, just a stop, that's all it was."

John stepped into the road and held up his hand. Seconds later a shot shattered the stillness of that bright February day and John crumpled to the ground. Paul's first thought was that a member of the patrol must have accidentally fired a shot. "I remember thinking I can smell cordite and my first thought was 'somebody's had a f*****g ND (negligent discharge)'. Because it seemed so close, this smell of cordite; it was so strong."

Very quickly, though, Paul realised that it had NOT been an ND, but a sniper attack.

"I went straight over to John and I think a couple of the soldiers came over as well and they were for dragging him in to the side of the road but I didn't want to move him. To me, moving him was worse than leaving him where he was.

"I was looking for a wound. I was looking for an entry and an exit wound. And all I saw was a small hole in his back. I was talking to John and I was holding him and saying 'Stay with us John.' And he asked 'Am I hit?'. I said 'You are but it'll be ok'.

"I can't remember if he said 'I'm going to die' or not but he just went, there and then, literally died right there in my arms."

Paul had been in combat many times and seen terrible things in war-torn places like Iraq and Afghanistan. But this was the first time a comrade had died in his arms.

"It's difficult for people to understand, because most people think of what they see on television when somebody dies. For me there is no light in the eyes. When a person dies and you look in their eyes there's nothing. That's the difference between somebody being alive and somebody being dead; there's no light, they're gone; the soul has gone, whatever you want to call it. What was there is just not there anymore. Just a corpse, a husk. Even though his body was still warm, when I looked in his eyes I knew there was nothing there."

John had become the sniper's second victim. He was thirty years old and single.

"It wasn't a Barrett round that hit John. It was 7.62mm – an AK47 round. We learned later that it was two guys in a car in the village looking down on us. They were in the boot and they just pushed down the number plate which had been made into a flap. They must have been reasonably close; that's why I could smell cordite. And in all the melee they probably just pulled out and quietly drove away."

The round hit John in the back and the post-mortem examination revealed it had just clipped his heart as it travelled through his body. "The trauma to his heart just stopped it," explained Paul.

"I just saw a small hole in the back. Bearing in mind we were in those green raincoats, you know those normal sort of dark patrol coats. We didn't wear body armour down there because it was way too heavy for what we had to do and became a hindrance really with the pack on our back."

Now, the team's training kicked in. "We just went into automatic mode. We got on to the to the radio for support. The doctor from Crossmaglen Health Centre came screaming down to the checkpoint in his car before anybody else had arrived and some of the lads, being understandably jittery, were raising their rifles. He jumped out, flung his hands in the air and shouted 'I'm a doctor'. He went over to John but pronounced life extinct; he was gone. Then the Royal Scots came out. They put a cordon in and things went into the normal mode for a fatal incident – forensics, CID and all that stuff.

"When the Lynx came down, I said I'm going to accompany the body, I'm going to accompany John to Daisy Hill. So I did. I got in with John and when we landed at Daisy Hill there was a CID officer I knew. They took over the body, put it in the morgue and I was taken down to Corry Square police station.

"The CID officers said 'Look, maybe you should wait 24 hours but I said I can't, I need to get my statement in now while it is completely fresh in my mind. I didn't want to chance contaminating it with any other thing. So I sat in the CID office and I wrote my statement out because it was fresh in my mind." With his statement complete, Paul was again given the chance to go home but he said no; he wanted to go back to Crossmaglen. "The guys are sitting there, my team is sitting there, and they haven't a clue what's really happened. I need to go back there so that they know what's going on and I need to go back for me as well.

"So I eventually got back in and sat down with the guys and we had a debrief and that was therapeutic as far as I was concerned. Didn't change anything but was just therapeutic. And that's what professional counsellors can't understand really. You've got to listen to the men and women on the ground. They're the ones who experience it.

"For some reason or another, in all the danger that I've been in over the years, I seem to have emerged unscathed and you're left to face what's called 'imposter syndrome' and 'survivor's guilt'.

"Many times I have thought about how, if I had stood up, it could and would have been me. But I don't beat myself up over it. I don't do that because you can't change the past. I mourn things, but I can't change anything so, as I say, I try not to beat myself up about it. Because we know the danger that we are in, it's almost as if we know there is a good chance one of us won't survive.

"You don't think about that because if you did, well, you wouldn't do it.

"I think that people who joined the RUC, by and large, knew what they were doing. Even the young constables, because they're young, tend to have this gung ho attitude. That is soon put out of them. That's not to say they're not silly any more but it is boxed away in a different part of their lives when they are off duty. When you have faced the reality of hundreds of people trying to f*****g kill you in a really bad riot situation, you have no illusions about what is coming your way.

"But it doesn't stop you and that's why I think the RUC in particular was a force like no other in the world because there was no other force in the world that had to experience that and yet remained intact and honourable and not corrupt. I'm not saying there wasn't the odd bad apple but it was certainly not the norm.

"I have always found it to be honourable and without corruption. Pretty much the most incorrupt force in the world. I've always thought that and I was proud to be in it. If I had believed there was corruption I wouldn't have been in it and neither would any of the guys I knew. If they had thought one of their colleagues was in a paramilitary organisation, they would have shopped him at the drop of a hat. They wouldn't have anything to do with it."

The Map

6

Massacre

You think you know a story.

You think, after forty four years, that nothing about that story can shock you.

But then you talk to a man who was there, who stooped to remove ammo clips from the pockets of corpses, still smouldering so much that the fear was the bullets would go off, who tried to match body parts to bodies like it was some sort of grotesque jigsaw.

And that man tells you a detail you'd never heard before; a nightmare vision which he has carried for decades.

You CAN be shocked…

Narrow Water Murders, Warrenpoint, Co. Down, August 27, 1979.

Kevin*, a detective constable with the CID, answers the phone. The message is urgent, economic, efficient.

"There've been explosions at Narrow Water, multiple casualties, get there."

And he did; within minutes. Kevin had seen violent death up close distressingly often. But this was carnage on a scale he had never experienced – few had.

Two bombs, separated by just over half an hour, caused what would remain the British army's biggest loss of life in a single incident in Northern Ireland.

Just about every aspect of the Narrow Water attack has been explored and explained over the years. We know where the bombs were made, who planned the attack, who carried it out and how they did it.

Soldiers and police officers search through the twisted wreckage of the lorry trailer that contained one of two massive bombs which exploded within a short time of each other in August 1979 at Narrow Water near Warrenpoint. This was the army's biggest loss of life in a single incident during the 'Troubles'. Eighteen soldiers were killed, all but two of them members of the Parachute Regiment.

What I'm interested in here is what it looked like through Kevin's eyes, eyes which – although he was still a relatively young man – had seen so much; and what this tells us about the unique set of difficulties faced by detectives who worked the area defined by 'the Map'.

Narrow Water, as the name suggests, is a narrow inlet from the sea (Carlingford Lough) which eventually meets Newry Canal. It separates Northern Ireland from the Republic of Ireland. On the northern side, a dual carriageway runs parallel to the water. And it was along this picturesque stretch of road that three British Army vehicles were travelling when the first blast happened. The IRA had placed an 800lb fertiliser bomb on a flatbed trailer, then hidden it with straw bales. This trailer was parked at the side of the road. As the last of the three military vehicles passed it, the bomb was set off by remote control by members of the IRA watching from the thick woods across the river. Six of the eight soldiers in the lorry were killed. It was twenty to five.

The army responded quickly, but predictably. And that predictability was to prove fatal. Anticipating that senior officers would set up an incident control point exactly where they did, the IRA had left a second bomb of a similar size. At 12 minutes past five, it exploded killing 12 more soldiers. Three men were standing almost on top of the second bomb and were virtually vaporised by the blast. They were Major Peter Fursman of the Parachute Regiment, Lieutenant-Colonel David Blair of the 1st Scottish Highlanders and his radio operator Lance-Corporal Victor MacLeod.

The memories, for Kevin, stay vivid and close.
"Really, just about nothing was found of Col Blair. Major Fursman's skull was found in the river by police divers and all they recovered of the radio operator, Lance-Corporal MacLeod, was the butt of his Browning pistol.

"I was given the job of numbering each of the 14 bodies that remained at the scene. I numbered them from 1 to 14 but it turned out there were two number sevens, which I numbered as seven and 7a. They were both the same man but his upper half had been removed to hospital after showing signs of life. Not surprisingly, though, he was beyond saving."

Soldiers and police officers search through the twisted wreckage of the lorry trailer that contained one of two massive bombs which exploded within a short time of each other in August 1979 at Narrow Water near Warrenpoint.

No matter how detailed and informative written accounts of an event like this might be, hearing first hand from someone who was there takes you to another level of understanding. There is something perhaps in the voice, perhaps in the eyes, or maybe in the body language that seems to bring you, just a little way, into their secret world, gives you a brief glimpse of the horror they gazed upon. For a few moments you imagine you can feel the dead weight of the trauma carried by those who can never set it down.

Then Kevin tells me that detail I had never heard before.

"The next morning, they had to get the helicopter to come down and fly low to the ground on the castle side of the road to blow down all the body parts that were still hanging in the trees: fingers, bits of skin, bits of head hair etc which were collected then by SOCOs on the ground. I can see it all clearly to this day."

So Kevin and his colleagues were faced with murder on a massive scale. But how do you even start an investigation when you really have no direction to go? The suspects aren't even in your jurisdiction.

"The old 'A' squad were sent up to help us; they were based out of Belfast and were deployed when needed at murders right across Northern Ireland. These guys had seen it all, but I think even they were taken aback with the whole thing."

Just two days after the bombing which killed so many of their colleagues, the Parachute Regiment returned to Narrow Water. This never before published photograph shows members of the regiment on parade, primarily to honour their dead colleagues but with a sense of defiance also.

There was, at this time, very little – in fact, let's face it - NO recognition of the psychological impact that being involved with an incident like this can have. When Kevin called at Ballykinlar Camp the following morning, he was surprised by the level of normality: children going to school, life seemingly just going on.

"I mentioned this to the RSM who was particularly old school in his approach. He just looked at me and said: 'We are the British Army; we expect to take casualties."

So, problem number one for detectives like Kevin: the sheer number of cases. He handled dozens of murders. One of his colleagues was in charge of 141 murder investigations in a four-year period. The pace was brutal.

"The difficulty in that South Armagh area was that you could never get witnesses. Nobody would talk to you; everybody was scared. I mean when you are calling at a house hoping the occupant will give you a witness statement and outside in their garden are heavily armed soldiers there to protect you from the people you want them to speak out against; soldiers who will leave when you leave, well, it doesn't exactly fill them with confidence."

The Miami Showband Murders, Co Down, July 31, 1975

Of course, the IRA were not the only paramilitaries operating in this area, and indeed, some of the most shocking murders were carried out by loyalists, including what became known as the Miami showband Massacre.

The Miami were one of Ireland's leading showbands in the early '70s. At a time when violence, and the ever-present threat of violence, meant many bands chose to avoid Northern Ireland altogether, they kept playing gigs north of the border, attracting huge crowds desperate for a little respite, however brief, from the pervasive horror of the Troubles

On the night of the attack, they had played in Banbridge and were on their way back to Dublin. They hadn't travelled far, hadn't even reached Newry, just into the area covered by 'the Map', when their VW minibus was stopped at what was then a very familiar sight, an army checkpoint. Or so they believed.

In fact, they had been stopped by a UVF gang disguised as soldiers and with murderous intent. They had brought with them a 10lb bomb and an evil plan.

This much we know:

The gang's plan was to appear to be carrying out a routine search of the minibus and to use this as an opportunity to secrete the bomb, which was contained in a briefcase, under a seat. They would let the band members re-board the bus, still believing they had simply been briefly detained at a routine army checkpoint. The bomb would explode somewhere en route to Dublin, killing everyone in the vehicle. It would appear that members of the band had been moving explosives across the border. Pressure would increase on the authorities to try to seal the border, thereby cutting off potential IRA escape routes. A couple of things have always troubled me about this theory: if you were trying to paint the band members as IRA sympathisers who were smuggling a bomb, would you not have needed the bomb to be travelling in the opposite direction? It would have made no sense for them to be carrying a primed bomb OUT of Northern Ireland. Secondly, the UVF would not have been known for 'big picture' strategic attacks like this supposedly was.

In his book 'the Dirty War' Martin Dillon claims the band were also targeted because they were popular within

The 'Miami Showband Massacre

the nationalist community. It would be foolish indeed to rule out the possibility of the familiar UVF motivation of sectarian bloodlust even if two of the band members were Protestants, although only one of them, Brian McCoy, was travelling in the minibus that evening.

Over the years I have been offered various other 'reasons' for the why and where of the attack from a personal grudge against McCoy, held by the attack organiser, Robin 'the Jackal' Jackson to the location being chosen by Jackson because it was on the Buskhill Road which was similar enough to 'Bus Kill' for him to apparently find it, in some sick way, amusing. These theories are beyond proving.

To return to what we know for sure.

The aftermath of the murders that became known as the 'Miami Showband Massacre'. Loyalist paramilitaries posing as British soldiers shot dead three members of the popular showband after stopping them at a bogus checkpoint. Two of the gang also died when a bomb they were attempting to hide on the band's minibus exploded.

The bomb exploded prematurely. The two UVF members who were in the process of planting it, Harris Boyle and Wesley Somerville were killed instantly, both decapitated. Boyle and Somerville were members of both the UVF and the UDR as were two other members of the gang who were later convicted. Another of the killers, also convicted, was a former member of the UDR.

At least one member of the gang spoke with an English accent. It has been suggested that this man (or possibly men) arrived on the scene by car AFTER the minibus had been stopped and that his/their arrival dramatically changed the atmosphere.

After the bomb exploded, the gang opened fire on the band members in a bid, presumably, to kill any potential witnesses. It was a savage, merciless act. Fran O'Toole, the band's lead singer, was shot more than 20 times, mostly in the face. The other two victims, Brian McCoy and Tony Geraghty, were also hit numerous times. Incredibly, two men were to survive; saxophone player Des McAlea and bass guitarist Stephen Travers. Des was blown into the undergrowth and lay motionless next to a burning hedge until the gunmen left. Stephen Travers had been seriously wounded but lay still and pretended to be dead. He was lying beside the body of Brian McCoy. In a moment of unimaginable terror one of the gang kicked Brian McCoy's body to make sure he was dead but left Stephen, apparently convinced he couldn't have survived as he had been shot with 'dum-dum' bullets.

I have met and talked with Stephen Travers several times over the years. He is a courageous and honourable man who is driven by a desire to know the truth of what happened that night.

But it is at this point that narratives diverge. Stephen, Des and the families of other victims believe the leader of the Mid-Ulster UVF, Robin Jackson, was, at the time of the killings, a Special Branch agent, a position supported in a report by the Historical Enquiries Team (HET). They also believe that the undercover soldier Captain Robert Nairac, was present at the massacre meaning that, by extrapolation, British Military Intelligence had a hand in what happened.

But Kevin too is a courageous and honourable man. When he talks about the investigation, it is with the quiet, calm assurance of a man galvanised with the simple truth.

When asked if Robert Nairac was there, he gives, with total confidence, the unambiguous answer: "Robert Nairac was never there."

He believes a member, or maybe members, of the gang put on an English accent, knowing that the band members would be more relaxed if they believed they were dealing with the regular British Army rather than the UDR.

"Nairac wasn't there; he had nothing to do with that.
"We had people arrested very quickly. And we had 'the Jackal' in too."

The 'Jackal' was a nickname given to Robin Jackson. "When the HET looked at the case, what they told the families and survivors was that the Jackal was a police informant and that his handlers had got him offside virtually straightaway and that it was several months before the police were able to interview him.
"But that's not correct because he was interviewed within days of the murders. I mean, he didn't say anything; he was questioned and released."

Most of the records relating to this were destroyed in a mortar attack on Bessbrook police station, but Kevin says some do still exist at the Complaints and Discipline branch.

"Jackson actually made a complaint against two police officers, claiming that he was assaulted. The two officers were convicted at Newry Magistrate's Court but were acquitted on appeal.

"The murders were on the 31st of July and in early September, only really about a month later, the two police officers were interviewed by Complaints and Discipline. If Jackson had not been interviewed and made the complaint before that then that would never have taken place.

"The HET went about things the wrong way. Some of them were good people who were quite willing to listen. But some of them just didn't want to know about anything at all. They formed their own opinion and just put that on paper and certainly convinced the families of the victims accordingly."

This book is by no means meant to be a re-investigation of the Miami Showband Massacre and the events that surrounded it. I detail all of this merely to illustrate another difficulty faced by detectives like Kevin in this area at this time. It can perhaps be best summed up by that old adage: "Anybody who isn't confused here, doesn't really know what's going on."

This was a filthy 'war' in which many people did unspeakable things. Some of them were rogue members of the security forces. But there remained many courageous men and women with the character and the integrity to put themselves in harm's way every single day, to risk their lives in order to protect others and simply to do the right thing.

Kevin says he never felt there was any interference with, or attempt to influence, any of his investigations. "As a percentage, I'd say we caught more loyalists than republicans. But, in reality, it didn't matter to us. I can look anyone in the eye and say 'I did my best, on every case'. If the victim was Protestant or Catholic, we dealt with it, loyalist or republican, we dealt with it, a police colleague or a total stranger, we dealt with it.

"And we rooted out any wrong-doers within our ranks – the moment they were uncovered."

This was despite the workload, the constant extreme danger, the almost total lack of witnesses and the, possible or actual, misinformation that seemed to be a constant presence right across 'the Map'.

* Name withheld

The Map

7

Blue on Blue

"People sleep peacefully in their beds at night only because rough men stand ready to do violence on their behalf."
– George Arnott

When the shooting ended, there was silence; silence like Michael* had never experienced, silence like an abyss, that seemed to swallow anything and everything in its path. The gun smoke and smell of cordite were drifting away. The police officers had shot the streetlights out so everything was in darkness. Into this silent dark stepped one of the gunmen, his hands held high above his head. It was his voice that finally broke the stranglehold of the silence and brought a horrifying realisation for Michael and his colleagues. The accent was English, the words were almost unbearable. "You've made a dreadful mistake lads, you've made a dreadful mistake."

As the Cold War entered its final phase in the 1980s, NATO troops taking part in military exercises used to "fight" the armies of the Warsaw Pact. Of course, the actual Soviet Union and its allies were not likely to make themselves available, so a selection of NATO troops

would stand in for them. They could be recognised as 'the enemy' by the red pennants they flew. The NATO troops playing the part of themselves, meanwhile, would fly blue pennants. Any action by western soldiers that harmed their own comrades became known as a 'Blue on Blue' incident. Away from the theoretical world of war games, the phrase transferred into common usage in the real world among almost all NATO armies as a somewhat euphemistic, way of describing the horrific, traumatic act of accidentally harming or even killing your comrades.
In the Northern Ireland troubles, such incidents were surprisingly rare. But they did happen.

It was 1967 when Michael strode into the RUC training depot in Enniskillen, a "fresh-faced 18-year-old who was ready to sort the world out." But, as he puts it, his life as a policeman, in the traditional sense, was cut very short.

Rioting erupted in Derry around protests organised by the Civil Rights Movement. Michael recalls: "A lot of single men were conscripted into what were known as Reserve Force Platoons.

"They consisted of one head constable, as it was in those days, five sergeants and about 30 constables. I was sent to Gough barracks in Armagh to join Number Eight Reserve Platoon."

The Hunt report, which was set up to look into perceived bias in policing in Northern Ireland, was published in 1969 and, as part of a restructuring, the Reserve Force Platoons became the Special Patrol Group (SPG).

"At that stage we were disarmed and there was a bit of controversy about that because we were expected to do prison escorts and one thing and another with no weapons. So a minor rebellion took place within the ranks and after a bit of deliberation we were given the arms back."

And it was as a member of the SPG that Michael became involved with the 'Blue on Blue' incident, one of three separate, traumatic events that punctuated his time in the RUC, any one of which would have had most people seriously reviewing their choice of career.

It was March 20, 1974.

"We were doing a double car patrol in two armoured Ford Cortinas. There was a Sergeant and three constables in each of the cars and we were doing what was known as parallel patrolling in South Armagh. About nine o'clock, I had gone back to the station with my crew for a break. And we were sitting in Armagh station listening to the radio on a portable transmitter. We got a message from our other patrol which was still out on the ground. They had made a contact (radio shorthand for an engagement with the enemy) at a place called Shaw's lake, just outside the village of Glenanne."

The other crew, it seemed, had come across an illegal vehicle checkpoint. A yellow Commer minibus was parked at the side of the road and several armed men were standing around it.

"The other patrol stopped short and shone lights down on these men and challenged them. The result was that they were met with a volley of fire from the armed men down the road. So they engaged them and one of these guys was shot dead. And another one was injured.

At that stage, we felt it was a terrorist attack and it was put out across the air as a terrorist engagement."

Shaw's Lake Glenanne where the first shooting took place
Photo: Greg Haire

Michael's unit reacted immediately. "As far as we were concerned, we were on our way to give support to our colleagues who were out there and in real danger. We were driving through Markethill in the direction of Glenanne when we had another radio message saying that a Land Rover had been hijacked by the remnants of the gang and was heading back towards Markethill.

"Now, it was obvious that we were going to meet this vehicle on the road so we were fully switched on and alert. This would be a fight for our lives.

"When we came round the bend into the village of Mowhan, sure enough there was the Land Rover parked with its nose in against the telephone kiosk at the post office. The guy was standing – I can still see it as plain as day - in civilian clothing with a hand gun - using the telephone. There was another guy in denims, standing at the back of the Land Rover with a sub-machine gun. We were going at a fair pace at the time - I remember our driver screeched the car to a halt. The next thing there was a volley of fire from these guys at the post office and our vehicle was hit several times.

"Another constable and I were armed with Lee Enfield 303 rifles. We were sitting in the back seat and the two of us got out of the vehicle on the near side, keeping the car between us and the gunmen. And we returned fire. The guy from the telephone kiosk had run out and lay down behind the nearside wheel of the Land Rover and was firing on us from that position. I can remember seeing the muzzle flashes so I focused my attention on those and I fired seven rounds at the front wheel. The other constable also fired a few shots. The result of that was that the guy who was standing with the sub-machine gun jumped behind the wall of the post office and the other guy was shot dead.

"We shot the streetlights out just to darken the place in case there were more terrorists about."

It was then that the silence descended and a short time later the terrible realisation of what had happened began to dawn.

What HAD actually happened was a series of mistakes and unfortunate coincidences.

As a matter of course, the SPG patrols had, before setting off, checked in with the army's control room. On this occasion, they were told there were no military patrols in South Armagh. And, to some extent, that was true. But what the control room failed to mention was that there WAS a group of armed soldiers in civilian clothes moving around the area.

They had been on a mid-tour relief break in Germany and were being dropped off in small groups at various police stations along the border. While they were actually based at Gosford Castle, a few soldiers were assigned to provide extra security at each of those stations deemed to be vulnerable to attack. This, again, was in the wake of the Hunt Report when police officers were not, as a rule, heavily armed.

The soldiers were being transported in the yellow Commer van which the first police patrol encountered at Shaw's Lake. It had broken down. Understandably nervous in an area which was seeing a lot of IRA activity around this time, several of the soldiers stood armed and alert while the others attempted to find a solution to their uncomfortable problem.

An IRA checkpoint in South Armagh.

Suddenly they were illuminated by car headlights. Men with strong Ulster accents were roaring instructions at them. They had to make a split second decision. They made it - and opened fire on their 'attackers' who fired back. From this point on, confusion reigned. It was going to be almost impossible to regain control of the rapidly deteriorating situation.

A soldier in the King's Hussars, Michael Francis Herbert, lay dead. He was a married father of one from Prestwick in Scotland. He was 31. One of his comrades was injured. When a 'civilian' Land Rover which had been dispatched to help recover the Commer arrived, the remaining soldiers clambered into it and fled towards Markethill as fast as they could, still believing they had come under attack from terrorists. With no means of radio communication, they decided to try to contact their base from a phone box in the tiny village of Mowhan. And we know what happened next: another firefight and another dead soldier. This time it was 36-year-old Michael J Cotton, again from the King's Hussars.

"From the moment our guys at the first scene misread the situation and thought it was a hijacking, it was just one unfortunate incident after another, the domino effect if you like. The two police cars that night were both red Cortinas; albeit one was a slightly lighter shade of red than the other. The soldiers probably thought, when they saw the second car, that it was the same one that had been involved in the previous incident and when they saw us decided they were going to get their shots in first. It was so unfortunate the whole thing."

Michael recalls how he and his colleagues, devastated by what had happened asked to be allowed to attend the soldiers' funerals. "We wanted to go to them but our authorities wouldn't allow us. But there was a representation from the outfit that we belonged to. It was just an awful situation. These guys were there to do the same job as us and by a series of terrible coincidences two of them end up dead."

Not surprisingly, the identity of these soldiers and what they were doing that night, was the subject of much misplaced speculation. Republican sources were convinced they were actually members of the SAS or some part of the army's secretive intelligence-gathering operations. As so often with conspiracy theories, the truth was a lot more prosaic – and for the army and the RUC – tragic.

"There was a court case down in Belfast obviously and an inquest and at that time the Attorney General absolved us of any blame. But it is still something that I have had to live with over the years.

"Always after that, I didn't like carrying a firearm. It was very difficult, a situation that was made worse many years later when we had an unfortunate incident at home. It was a Sunday afternoon and I was heading out to start duty at three o'clock. I was going out through the back door and I had a clean shirt and my Ruger revolver with me. The front doorbell rang just then, so I set them down on the worktop in the kitchen and went to let a friend of ours in through the front door.

The next thing I heard a bang coming from the kitchen. I ran in and my son was lying behind the kitchen door with blood coming out of his mouth. And I thought 'Oh my goodness, he's shot himself'. But what had happened was, there was a wee guy, a four or five year old boy, had come in uninvited from next door, had seen the revolver and lifted it and unfortunately my son had walked into the kitchen and the boy just shot him. The round struck my son on the lip and went out through his cheek. Thankfully, he survived, but, as you can imagine, weapons were not a very popular thing in our house."

Michael also survived an IRA attempt to murder him at his home.

"Fortunately, the Almighty had his hand on me that night and it came to nought."

It was in the early 90s. Michael was working the late shift in the control room at Armagh police station. Unbeknown to him, at his home a few miles away, the IRA too were about their work.

By their grisly timetable, he should have already been murdered, he should have been lying dead outside his home cut down without mercy by a hail of bullets fired from an automatic assault rifle. But instead he was still sitting, safe and sound, in the control room.

"An incident had occurred at a factory near Armagh and I started to co-ordinate it. Now, the unwritten rule was that if you started something you finished it before you terminated your duty. So I was involved with that incident and as a result I was running late."

Just after 11:30, his wife rang him on the direct line into the control room to tell him that their house was under attack. There had been a burst of automatic gunfire through the front window.

"I went to pieces on the other end of phone. I never felt as impotent in my life. There I was, stuck a few miles away from my own home which was being attacked and I actually heard the second burst of machine-gun fire over the phone. At that stage, my inspector had come into the control room and had learned what was going on. There were vehicles dispatched and another operator was called up to relieve me.

"It transpired that what had happened was the IRA had set up an ambush for me at the back of our garage at home. My children had pet rabbits at the time and there were two gates in the yard where they had put up planks to stop the rabbits escaping. And these guys had obviously got a bit anxious because I was late. They expected that the job would be done by this stage and they were lying behind the garage for maybe half an hour. Clearly, they got anxious. Some of them came down towards the house to see what was going on and accidentally knocked the plank down. My wife heard the noise and switched on the outside security system which had been switched off because she had been expecting me in. She didn't want me lit up as I arrived so she would have turned the system off and then, after I was in, switched it back on again. So whenever she heard the noise and put the lights back on again it obviously spooked them. They ran but, as they did, they fired two full magazines through the living room window".

Within minutes, the garden was flooded with Scenes of Crime Officers and detectives – EXACTLY as the IRA thought it would be. About half an hour after they had deliberately revealed their presence, a bomb planted by the IRA gang and containing 6lbs of Semtex wrapped with shrapnel exploded in the garden.

"The plan had been to murder me, then, whenever the responding units arrived, to kill them also.

"But not only that; they also had a 1,000lb bomb in a hay trailer on a nearby road because they knew that police responding to an incident on that side of the town would be coming in from that direction. Whenever the police car went past, they heard a bang and it was just the detonator going off. The whole lot didn't go.

"So it was a well organised attack but fortunately for everyone involved it went, as the IRA would see it, wrong. Nobody was seriously hurt. The worst injury that night was a ruptured eardrum. That time, I certainly questioned whether or not I should stay in Northern Ireland but I was in the fortunate position of winding down towards retirement. Whenever that incident happened, I had 28 ½ years service. We were moved immediately. The whole family was evacuated to St Andrews convalescent home in Harrogate and we stayed there until the Christmas break of that year."

Michael believes it was an encounter with a high-profile republican that had marked him out as a target. "About two years, possibly, before the attack on our house, I arrested the infamous Dessie Grew at Lislasly, between Loughgall and Moy. It was on the grounds of a report that we had received from the UDR.

"They had stopped a car (I believe it was an Austin Princess) driven by a guy who they felt was acting suspiciously. He was stopped and checked but nothing was found and he was allowed to go. But the UDR hung about the area and the next thing two guys emerged. It was Dessie Grew and another man. They weren't armed but they were in combats and whenever further enquiries were made it appeared that this car was hanging about to pick them up. We put two and two together and reckoned that they were targeting someone. And the person that we thought they were targeting was Reggie Williamson."

Reggie Williamson, a part-time reserve officer was later killed. A booby trap bomb exploded under his car as he drove away from a pub owned by his sister in the County Tyrone village of Moy. But one thing we do know for certain is that Dessie Grew was not involved. He was shot dead by the SAS two years before Reggie Williamson's murder.

He was, however, very much alive and, according to the police, very much active within the IRA, on the night he and his colleagues were arrested by Michael.

"I remember it well; the young guy who was driving was panicking and he said to Grew; what do I do, what do I do? And Grew told him 'you shut your mouth and that's it'.

"So the three of them were taken to Gough Barracks and the car was there also to be searched by engineers. Grew and the other guy with him said nothing for the entire four or five days or whatever it was. But the driver was young, inexperienced and under pressure. And lo and behold he broke and he took the murder of a grandfather and granddaughter at Benburb police station. There was an RPG seven fired at Benburb police station and they used the station crest as their aiming point. There were two civilians driving past just at that time; a grandfather and his grand daughter and they were both killed.

"Well, this guy took that. So out of that we ended up getting a conviction for a double murder and maybe, as I was the one who made the arrests, from then on, I became a target for Grew.

"I was also targeted going to church. I was brought in by Special Branch and told to change my routine because, when you fell into any kind of pattern, it was very easy for the terrorists to target you.

"That was how we lived then, checking for bombs under the car, not falling into predictable patterns of behaviour et cetera. Abnormal became our normal. Whenever I came off the police, I had to get counselling and I remember the doctor telling me how I had lived for 30 years on adrenaline and how, for all that time, there had been situations that used up the surplus adrenaline. But he said that when I had retired I simply didn't have that. My body was still producing adrenaline but then it became a depressant.

"But at the end of the day, I'm lucky; I made it through to retirement. So many of my colleagues didn't."

*Name withheld.

The Map

8

The Detective

"The Past is a foreign country; they do things differently there." - L P Hartley

The visitor stood shielding his eyes and gazing across South Armagh. The lush green fields contrasted with the dusty, dry heat of his homeland at this time of year. His questions would have to keep until the roar of the Lynx helicopter which had brought him to this spot faded.

It had deposited him on one of ten watchtowers built along the South Armagh border by the army. As the Lynx disappeared back towards Bessbrook, the visitor's attention turned to an information board, much like one you might see at a popular beauty spot. On it, he could trace the outline of the surrounding mountains, he could recognise landmarks and he could see a little forest of red arrows indicating various locations.

"What are these?" he asked the detective accompanying him.

"Those show the homes and properties belonging to the leaders and members of the IRA and bases used by them."

The visitor's eyes widened. He turned, genuinely perplexed, towards his host and asked: "Why then are they allowed to stand?"

But that, even in the darkest days, was simply not how things were done here. Instead, every death had to be investigated by detectives who had to painstakingly build cases, as best they could, in the standard way.

Viewed from the safety and comfort of our modern world, it's easy to criticise the police investigations at the height of the Troubles and difficult to remember, or even imagine, the pressure that those charged with trying to solve these crimes were under. In the seventies and eighties the 'thin green line' was stretched to its very thinnest as Northern Ireland teetered time and again on the edge of the abyss; all-out civil war.

Help from a public paralysed by fear was almost non-existent, evidence gathering often had to be undertaken in hostile areas where the investigators' own lives were in constant danger and the workload was immense as the paramilitaries relentlessly racked up victim after victim.

But for a society to keep functioning, one of the basic requirements is the upholding of the rule of law. Every murder had to be investigated. Here then, by way of illustration, are excerpts from the notebooks and diaries kindly made available to me, of just one detective. I'll call him Peter. I have included, where I can, a few brief details of the victims and how they met their deaths, partly as an illustration of the pressure Peter and his colleagues were under, partly as a reminder that these were real fathers, mothers, husbands, brothers, sisters, friends. They would never know how hard Peter would try to find their killers, never know how he and others like him would put themselves in harm's way as part of that search, never know if their killers were brought to justice.

Soldiers search for Thomas Cochrane, a part-time member of the Ulster Defence Regiment (UDR) who was abducted by the IRA in October 1982 as he travelled to work from his home near Bessbrook. Falling into the hands of the IRA was the biggest fear for any member of the security forces.

We begin exactly halfway through Northern Ireland's most bloody decade – the 1970s - and Peter's entry in his notebook for July 31, 1975:

"Involved in the investigation of the Miami Showband killings."

One of the most notorious and controversial incidents of the troubles. Three members of the hugely popular showband; lead singer Fran O'Toole, Trumpet player

Brian McCoy and Anthony Geraghty, were killed after their van was stopped at a bogus army checkpoint set up by the UVF between Banbridge and Newry. Two members of the UVF gang were also killed when a bomb they were attempting to hide in the band's bus exploded prematurely. It is widely accepted that the attack was organised by the notorious Loyalist paramilitary leader Robin 'the Jackal' Jackson and that his brother-in-law Samuel Fulton Neill was also involved. Neill was later shot dead outside a Portadown pub. He was shot in the head five times with Jackson - having apparently come to believe Neill was an informer - once again the chief suspect. The police believe Jackson was responsible for more than 50 killings. He died of cancer in 1998.

NUMBER OF DEATHS BEING INVESTIGATED 5

"September 1, 1975. Involved in the investigation of the murders of five persons in Tullyvallen Orange Hall."

Four people were killed when IRA gunmen burst into the remote Orange Hall in South Armagh. They were father and son William and James McKee, 80-year-old John Johnston and Nevin McConnell who managed a local livestock market. A fifth man, William George Herron, died from his injuries two days later in hospital. As two IRA members armed with machine guns sprayed bullets inside, others fired through the windows from outside. An explosive device was later found outside the hall where it had been left, presumably with the intention of killing more people as they fled or members of the security forces who turned up to help.

NUMBER OF DEATHS BEING INVESTIGATED 10

"January 6, 1976. Involved in the investigation into the murders of 10 persons at Kingsmills in County Armagh."

The killing of 10 Protestant workmen, in what became known as the Kingsmills Massacre, remains one of the most shocking incidents in the dark history of the Troubles. The men were travelling home from the textile factory where they worked when their minibus was stopped by gunmen. One of the workers was identified as a Catholic and told to 'run up the road'. Those left behind were lined up and shot.

The Kingsmills Massacre Memorial, erected at the scene on this isolated stretch of road in South Armagh
- Photo: Greg Haire

Only one man, Alan Black, survived. He had been shot up to 14 times (the extent of his injuries was such that doctors could not be totally certain about that number). I have known Alan for many years and have sat and listened to his first-hand account of that night more than once. The killings were claimed by a group calling itself the South Armagh Republican Action Force. It said they were in retaliation for the murders of members of the Reavey and O'Dowd families the night before. I have not added their deaths to the total here only because other detectives were involved with that investigation. As with Alan Black, however, I have also known Eugene Reavey (a brother of the victims) for many years and have heard first-hand about that night. What has always struck me is how pain, grief, trauma and everything else that comes with this sort of terrible violence does not differentiate between families. It rips them all apart.

An investigation by the Historical Enquiries Team many years later concluded that the South Armagh Republican Action Force was simply a cover name for the IRA.

NUMBER OF DEATHS BEING INVESTIGATED 20

"August 27, 1979, Involved with the investigation into the murder of 18 soldiers at Narrow Water."

From the end of August until October of '79, Peter was involved in inquiries in South Armagh into the Warrenpoint murders. This was the British Army's heaviest loss of life in a single incident during the troubles. eighteen soldiers were killed; six in an initial explosion and twelve in a follow-up blast, the IRA having successfully predicted just where responding soldiers would set up their defensive position.

NUMBER OF DEATHS BEING INVESTIGATED 38

"October 8 to 18, 1979. Involved in the investigation into the murder of Robert George Hawthorne."

Robert Hawthorne was a 39-year-old father of three. He was also a former member of the UDR and it was this that the IRA gave as its justification for killing him. He was shot as he parked his car outside a timber yard in Newry where he worked as a fork lift truck driver. A passenger with him was also slightly injured.

NUMBER OF DEATHS BEING INVESTIGATED 39

"January 2, 1980. Involved in the investigation into the murder of Samuel Lundy."

Another former member of the UDR, Mr Lundy was shot outside his home in Kingsmills as he arrived back from work. The IRA issued a statement in which they said Mr Lundy should have informed them when he left the UDR. Two brothers-in-law of Mr Lundy had been murdered in 1975. One of these was Robert Frazer, the father of the high profile loyalist campaigner, the late Willie Frazer.

NUMBER OF DEATHS BEING INVESTIGATED 40

Murder cases beyond the area covered by 'the Map' also had to be investigated.

"January 6, 1980. Involved in the investigation into the murders of three UDR soldiers in a bomb attack near Castlewellan."

The three soldiers, Robert Smith, James Cochrane and Richard Samuel John Wilson, died when a huge bomb planted under a bridge exploded as they drove over it in their Land Rover. It was triggered by a command wire from a derelict house 250 yards away. It left a crater 30 feet wide and 13 feet deep. The emergency services had to work waist-deep in water as mains pipes had been burst by the explosion. Four other soldiers were injured.

NUMBER OF DEATHS BEING INVESTIGATED 43

"February 11, 1980. Made inquiries at Lisnaskea re the murders of RUC officers Rose and Howe."

Winston Howe was 35 and a father of two. Joseph Rose was only 21. Like the UDR soldiers in Castlewellan, they were killed by a landmine hidden in a culvert. Again, it was detonated by remote control as their Land Rover drove over the culvert.

NUMBER OF DEATHS BEING INVESTIGATED 45

"March 7, 1980. Was part of the investigation into the murder of Henry Livingstone in Armagh."

Henry Livingstone was 38 and a former member of the UDR. The unmarried farmer lived with his elderly widowed mother.

NUMBER OF DEATHS BEING INVESTIGATED 46

"April 17, 1980. Conducted inquiries in Newtownbutler and Lisnaskea in relation to the murder of Victor Morrow."

Victor Morrow was yet another former member of the UDR. He was shot a short distance from his home as he walked to get a lift to work the night shift as a security officer at a factory in Lisnaskea. He was shot nine times in the back of the head.

NUMBER OF DEATHS BEING INVESTIGATED 47

"August 31, 1980. Conducted inquiries into the abduction of Wallace Allen in south Armagh."

Inevitably, the abduction inquiries soon became a murder investigation and a frantic hunt began for the body of the RUC reservist. That search ended almost a fortnight after he went missing while driving his milk lorry. It emerged that he had died from being shot in the head very shortly after being abducted. For Peter and his colleagues, these were particularly difficult and distressing cases.

I had intended to include a chapter in this book about officers who were abducted by the IRA, but such was the hurt and trauma endured by relatives of those particular victims that, even decades later, it's just too difficult and painful for them to talk about.

Two other police officers were to suffer a similar fate: William Turbitt and Louis Robinson, as well as a number of UDR soldiers.

Here, I will set down a few details on the two police officers.

Constable William Turbitt: When I called with William Turbitt's son, I had miscounted in my head. I had wrongly arrived at the idea that the man I was meeting had been six at the time of his father's abduction and murder. In fact, he had been 12. "I suppose you don't really remember that day," I ventured. A sadness reaching back through the decades filled his eyes as he replied simply:

"Oh I remember it, every second of it."

It was the worst fear of any officer serving in South Armagh – to be taken alive by the IRA. This would not be like being hauled into Gough or Castlereagh for questioning by the police. There would be no lawyers, no interview recordings, no getting home alive.

It was June 17, 1978, just shy of the longest day of the year. William Turbitt and his colleague, Constable Hugh McConnell, were driving near Sturgan's Brae just above the scenic Camlough Lake.

Those who knew Hugh McConnell invariably begin their recollections of him by describing what a talented footballer he was, having played for both Newry Town and the RUC. Indeed, in the one photograph I have of him, dated only 'mid seventies', he is posing alongside his colleagues and team-mates in the Bessbrook and Newry RUC team.

It was a 999 call from a member of the public that first raised the alarm. They said a police officer's body was lying beside the car. It was the body of Hugh McConnell. He had died instantly when the car was hit with more than 20 high velocity bullets fired by an IRA ambush team who had been lying in wait.

There was no sign of William Turbitt, a father of four. For his family, this marked the beginning of 12 days of suffering and a lifetime of grief.

The IRA claimed that, despite his injuries, they were able to "interrogate" him, but a later report by the state pathologist's office said such was the severity of his wounds that it was unlikely he would have survived for any length of time.

The following day, a Catholic Priest, Father Hugh Murphy from Ahoghill, was kidnapped and a caller to a radio station said he would be returned "in the same condition" as William Turbitt. He was, however, released unharmed after 12 hours. A number of police officers would be later convicted of involvement in his kidnapping.

Det Constable Louis Robinson: September 16, 1990. Louis Robinson, who was on long-term sick leave with depression, had been on a fishing trip to Dingle, County

Kerry, with five prison officers. They were returning home on the main Dublin to Belfast Road near the Killeen border crossing, known to the security forces as BCP 5, when their minibus was stopped just over the border in South Armagh and he was abducted. His body was found near the village of Belleeks three days later. His hands were bound behind his back and a hood placed over his head, a grisly fate normally reserved by the IRA for suspected informers within their own organisation.

We know what happened on the bus in some detail thanks to the first-hand accounts given by the prison officers who were with Constable Robinson.

The bus was initially stopped at what appeared to be a regular army vehicle checkpoint. Once it had come to a halt, masked and armed men appeared and it quickly became clear they already knew there was a police officer on board. One of the prison officers was told: "You're the black bastard." But he said he was a prison officer and his accuser moved on. Three of the prison officers managed to break free and escaped despite a shot being fired at them, but two of their colleagues were taken along with Detective Constable Robinson. The two were badly beaten before being released. For Constable Robinson, though, there was to be no mercy.

Earlier this year, I recorded a short series of interviews for this book with a retired detective, now deceased, called John.

John and his CID partner put themselves in harm's way that night as they made desperate (and not officially sanctioned) attempts to find any trace of Detective Constable Robinson.

John recalled: "When Louis Robinson was taken, the button was pushed so to speak and a lot of people went looking for him. It was obvious that once they had him, away he went into South Armagh. My partner and I signed out a couple of rifles from the armoury in Armagh. My partner knew the area because he had been a uniformed officer there at a time when the police were still using the roads. In my time, we always used helicopters. If you were going to Silverbridge or Cullyhanna or wherever, the fields just looked the same; you couldn't have picked out any particular road. So we drove down and began to look in all the possible dumping sites. This was on the same night, Gordon. In fact, it was only a short time after he had been taken."

John felt the timing of the IRA's operation as well as the optics of letting the two abducted prison officers go was for the benefit of those who controlled the paramilitaries' publicity machine.

"It was a war of attrition. You know as well as I do Gordon, better even, but that's what it was and it was meant to put the fear of God into people…….. which it did."

The pair were ordered to return to base once senior officers became aware of what they were doing.

"I remember they called us back because it was getting just far too dangerous for us. The only way we could do it was to look, physically, in the old hay sheds and stables and stuff like that. But, I mean, it was suicide. You were definitely scared. If you weren't frightened down there, you shouldn't have been down there; it's as simple as that."

All that aside, for Peter and his colleagues, the relentless, grim tally kept clicking upwards.

NUMBER OF DEATHS BEING INVESTIGATED 48

"January 16, 1981, Warrenpoint. Inquiries re the murder of Ivan Toombs"

There are few 'Troubles' killings we know more about now than the murder of Ivan Toombs. We know how he was targeted, how the murder was planned and carried out, who killed him and – in as far as anyone can say – why he was singled out. We even know how and why he survived a previous attempt on his life. And we know all

Ivan Toombs
Photo kindly supplied
by Paul Toombs

this because the one-time IRA member, turned informer, Eamon Collins, wrote about it in the opening chapter of his book Killing Rage.

Ivan Toombs was 42 and married with five children. He worked in the customs office in Warrenpoint, but was also a major in the UDR. Eamon Collins was also employed in the Customs office and worked, at times closely, with Ivan Toombs. The story of how he set up for murder this man who was never anything but good to him, a decent, hard-working family man, is a tough read, but offers an insight into the mind of people like Eamon Collins, how they rationalise their actions, how – in Collins' own words – he could "depersonalise a man so that his death could not touch me." How, you find yourself asking, could Collins arrange the bloody, violent, obscene death of the man about whom he writes: "The more I found out about him, the more admirable I found him. He was a man of simple tastes who behaved decently to all, the sort of man who would have rebuked anyone who made an anti-Catholic comment. I liked him and I felt, in other circumstances, we might have been friends."

Contrast that with his reaction to Ivan Toombs' murder when it eventually happened, a murder that would simply not have taken place were it not for him. "I did not think much about Toombs' fate as a human being, except that he had died as the result of a perfectly executed operation. I admit that I felt real satisfaction that we had been the first IRA unit at the start of the New Year to get a kill, a good kill. I had worked for two years to bring off this operation."

But of course, at this time, none of this was known to Peter or his colleagues. I include it here really only to serve as an illustration of just how difficult their job was. How did you catch someone like Collins; a highly intelligent man who was seemingly able to reconcile these diametrically opposed positions and present to the world as his true feelings either one depending only on who he was talking to and what he knew they wanted to hear. Catching the gunman also proved difficult as, although originally from Armagh, he was living, quite openly, across the border in Dundalk. Indeed, he lived just across the road from Dundalk Garda Station, apparently without fear of arrest.

NUMBER OF DEATHS BEING INVESTIGATED 49

"January 20, 1981. Involved in the investigation into the murder of Maurice Gilvarry."

Maurice Gilvarry was suspected by the IRA of being a police informer. The organisation came to believe that he had tipped off the security forces about a raid on Ballysillan postal depot in 1978 when the SAS shot dead three IRA members and an unconnected civilian. Gilvarry's body, beaten and bound, was dumped on a border road in south Armagh, the by-now familiar fate of all those suspected of informing. This was a nerve-wracking situation for the investigating police officers, aware as they were of the ever-present possibility that they themselves would become the target of further gun attacks or booby trap bombs.

NUMBER OF DEATHS BEING INVESTIGATED 50

"June 20, 1981, made inquiries re murder of Neal Quinn"

Neal Quinn became the 100th RUC officer to lose his life in the conflict when he was shot dead while having a drink in a Newry pub. The Catholic father-of-three was shot several times by two men wearing motorcycle gear.

NUMBER OF DEATHS BEING INVESTIGATED 51

Sadly, the 100th police death was to be far from the last.

The deaths, not just of police officers but of people from all walks of life, continued with depressing regularity, nowhere more so than in the area covered by 'the Map' where detectives like Peter would continue to struggle to get justice for the victims and some kind of closure for their loved ones.

The Map

9

A Matter of Life and Death

Part 1 - Death

"We meet our fate on the very road we took to avoid it"
– Anon

"When I became a man, I put away childish things"
– 1 Corinthians 13:11

The late May Bank Holiday, 1981. Christopher* was eighteen, little more than a child. The lads he had gone to school with were planning a day out, a day enjoying the spring sunshine, a day kicking a football round a park, chasing girls, maybe a few beers. There would be little to set this day apart from any other.

But for Christopher it was a day he would never forget.

Now retired after a long and very successful police career, he recalls every detail not just of that day but of the entire weekend. In those few days, he had to deal with the first death of a colleague, his first police funeral and the first time he saw someone die in a single moment of ferocious, brutal violence. The boy really had become a man.

"On the Thursday evening, I was starting the night shift - a seven-day cycle. I was sitting in the ops room. There were a few of us who were in a little bit earlier than usual.

"Reports started coming in of a shooting and it turned out that one of our guys coming to work had been shot dead. He was an older guy; he would have been the senior man in the section. I had only been there a few months so I hadn't really got in with him. Sort of 'keep the cub at a distance' you know. Anyway, he had been shot dead coming in to work so we obviously had all that to deal with."

The constable's funeral was on the Sunday, the first time Christopher had experienced first-hand the raw grief of a bereaved family, struggling to come to terms with their life-shattering loss while all around them the practised, choreographed perfection of the police band, the immaculately turned out senior officers with their swagger sticks tucked under their arms, the coffin draped in the Union Flag on which sat the police cap with its harp and crown badge.

A difficult and emotional day. But that night it was business as usual for Christopher and his colleagues.

"We were out driving about Newry as per normal. We drove through the Drumalane housing estate on the edge of town. We went out past the estate down on to the Omeath Road which takes you directly to the border crossing we knew as BCP (Border Crossing Point) 1.

At about three o'clock in the morning, Christopher spotted a car parked on the side of the road. "It was a mustardy-coloured Hillman Hunter and I said to the guys 'I think that's the car that was used in the shooting'. We drove down to the junction with the Omeath Road and what they called the line which took you back up onto the quay. We did a u-turn and got back close enough that we could see. Confirmed; that was the car, registration number and all still on it. So we closed the road off and called it in."

Within 15-20 minutes, the well-oiled security machine has moved in. Helicopters are dropping troops on all the areas of high ground. The military know what they're doing, the police know what they're doing; everything is happening just as it should – or so it seems.

"About six o'clock in the morning we're asked to go round to the top end of the cordon, up on the town side and let the boys there away. So we drive round and we come out onto the top side. That's where the ICP (Incident Control Point) is so we actually see the final stages of the ATO's (Ammunition Technical Officer) examination. We're standing back behind the ATO's truck, his team are there and the ATO himself is hoking about the car doing all the bits and pieces. Probably after about half an hour of that, he comes back up and he's declared the car clear."

The ATO is a 35-year-old Warrant Officer called Michael O'Neill.

"We were in a blue Mk IV armoured Cortina Sport and this ATO sits on the bonnet of our car. Bank holiday, May morning, sun shining. It's probably about half seven at this stage; helmet off, suit still on, smoking a cigarette. And he said to us that we could organise the recovery vehicle because the car was obviously going to have to go to Gough for the forensics guys to check it over so it would have to be lifted on to a low loader.

"Anyway I start chatting to this guy because I've never seen anything like this before. And it turns out he's from a town in England that I happened to know a little about so we chat for a while. Then, for whatever reason, he just walks back down to the car.

"I just remember watching him leaning into the car. The four doors are open, the bonnet's up and the boot is open. He'd done all that and obviously checked inside. And then just this explosion and the sound and the light and the heat. I mean the light from the explosion seemed to overpower the early morning sun, that's how bright this was. And the stuff raining down on us and that moment of silence. Then all of the screaming and shouting, everybody kicking into action. There were people running down to where the car had been. But there was nothing there. The car was gone, that side of the road was gone; I mean there was NOTHING there."

But this was no time to stand and stare and through the dust and debris, his ears ringing, Christopher became aware of a sergeant barking orders at him and a few other officers. "Come with me," he shouted.

"We ran down this bank down below where the explosion had happened to the edge of the housing estate. And we are basically searching for the body at this stage. And, as we're doing this, as we're going through this overgrown hillside area trying to find this ATO and there's military there too doing the same thing, some people in the housing estate – now this is half seven or a quarter to eight in the morning – some people are bombarding us with whatever they can get their hands on to try to stop us getting down to where he is.

"And we're taking hits, you know, rocks and bottles and anything that they can throw at us. But we find the body and it's intact, it's still in the suit but decapitated.

"And that is surreal. Never having seen anything like it, it's like a scene out of a movie that you're in. And I remember this big sergeant just standing up and saying 'listen guys, we're not leaving here until we find the head'.

"No matter what flack we were taking, we were finding that head. And within a short space of time the head was found. But those words never left me. It kind of wasn't the images of the body or the head that stayed with me, but the words of the sergeant with the rocks and bottles flying round him – 'We're not leaving here until we find that head'.

"And I can remember coming home that morning, eighteen years of age, and my mum had the breakfast made. It's probably about nine o'clock now and mum's sitting at the table while I have my breakfast and she asked if much had happened during the night. And I just ate my breakfast and said 'no, no, just a quiet night you know'. I finished my breakfast, went to bed, slept. Then you got up that night and you did it all over again. So that was my first experience of, first of all losing a colleague, and then – linked to the same incident – actually seeing somebody die. And the proximity of that guy – us having had a conversation two minutes earlier. And then the sergeant – so calm, no matter what was going on round us. The crowd were actually throwing bottles of urine at us as well. I mean we were getting it, we were getting it, and he just told us what we had to do in such a matter-of-fact way.

"I can still remember coming home and having that conversation, or lack of conversation, with my mum. I don't know if it was self-preservation or protecting her because she's watching you go out to work every night you know. I do think many years later, now, in my quiet moments, what must it have been like for my mum and dad? Me, going out every day – up those steps at our house and away to another shift in Newry. Because I

ATOs or Ammunition Technical Officers were the army's bomb disposal experts. While this 1981 photo was taken at an incident outside the area of 'The Map', it shows a typical operation for the ATO, in this case checking for secondary devices after two RUC men were killed by an IRA landmine.

know that if it was now, when I'm the parent, how hard that would be."

Part 2 – Life

Fast forward a few years and the 18-year-old lad fresh out of the depot, has very quickly grown into a serious and capable man.

This particular day, he and his colleagues have been given the rather innocuous task of delivering paperwork to the local courthouse in Newry.

"There had been a bomb in a Radio Rentals type shop in Market Square. I can't recall if it had been that day or the day before, but there'd been a bomb left and it had exploded and caused damage and the CID were round doing inquiries."

Unknown to the detectives, a team of IRA gunmen had taken over a flat in what was then North Street flats. "It gave them the high ground dominating that whole Trevor Hill, Market Street, Water Street area and was always considered by us to be a real death zone because, when you were in there, you were like a goldfish in a bowl. It was the scene of many attacks, shootings, drogue attacks whatever.

"So the CID arrive and are making some sort of inquiry. And one of the detectives walks up the street, out of the main shopping street and up a side street. The flats are looking straight down the side street. And the boys then open up on the CID and this young detective was actually shot. He was hit in the groin.

"We rush from the courthouse round to the bottom of Hill Street. And it's another one of those surreal moments. We drive into Hill Street which is like a crossroads and this is all happening up to the left hand side. And as we're driving in you can actually see the lumps coming out of the road; like divots coming out of the tarmac and the thud of the gunfire."

At this stage, Christopher and his colleagues didn't realise that this young detective had been hit and was lying out in the road.

"There were a few officers returning fire and whatnot. This boy was sort of at the back end of a car but he was certainly still in danger.

"The next thing is, from our right hand side, this police car comes racing up and comes to a sudden stop. And this - now famous - sergeant gets out and pulls his handgun, a revolver, with six rounds in it and he's running up this side street towards the gunfire and he fires off his six rounds and we can see roughly what's going on. We see him grab the detective, who knows, by the belt or whatever and he drags him in between two cars and he's reloading. And he's fired another six rounds. Meanwhile, the gun team decide to scatter. Everything calms down, the gunfire's over and this sergeant just walks off into the sunset type of thing – never to be recognised. Never to be invited to the palace or Hillsborough Castle to be decorated. And as famous as he was - people say it was madness or it was reckless - but I can tell you it was just outstanding courage and bravery. Unbelievable, unbelievable; with nothing more than a handgun with six rounds. The divots, as I said, were coming out of the road and he ran towards them and grabbed the young detective. He saved his life, no doubt about it. The detective lived and went on to serve a long career."

Christopher found ways to cope with the things he saw and experienced over the years, but he recognises that for many that was not a straightforward task.

"It's almost like a drug and I think that's what happens to a lot of guys who go off the job. The drug stops and then your problems start because you then have time to sit and think about these things and there's not another one coming in straight away that stops you thinking back.

"I mean it was constant. If you think about Newry, Corry Square in particular, we lost 16 officers in 16 weeks. And even setting those deaths aside, it was constant down there – incidents, deaths, incidents, deaths – and every time you went out, you knew what you were going out into and you were being told at briefings all the time, you know, 'close call yesterday'. This stuff was coming back in that you didn't realise had happened. It was coming in via the branch, you know.

Constant vigilance could make the difference between life and death for police officers on what was then the world's most dangerous beat.

"The branch would be saying to you 'the reason that you didn't get hit yesterday was because you looked sharp; you pulled up, you all got out, boys got in to cover. You looked like you knew what you were about and the gunmen just thought, 'nah, we'll come back another day; we'll take another crew'. The number of times we were debriefed on things like that, particularly in the MSU.

"South Armagh IRA were risk averse and I used to say to my guys 'it's all about appearance; you see if you get out and you look like you're on top of your game that day, those guys won't touch you, those guys will go away'. The attitude of those guys was 'if everything's not in our favour, we'll come back another day'. They're looking for the soft touch, they're looking for you know – the two boys in the car, one reading, the other sitting sleeping. And they'll think 'yeh, we'll take these boys today'. And that was always in mind; when you get out you look like you know what you're doing, you get into cover. It was a bit of self-preservation first of all and then there was the team preservation. Everybody doing their bit and who knows how many people survived because of that appearance."

Or could it be fate that decides who lives and who dies?

"There's always a story. In every incident, there's always a story. Guys that swapped shifts or changed seats. Like Paul Slaine (See chapter two) for example that night. His sergeant's baby boy not well, his sergeant has to go home and Paul gets into that seat.

"You don't realise it at the time, what you're doing, and it's strange because guys that got injured down there, who were off on the sick for short or long time, when those guys were offered transfers, they invariably turned them down and wanted to go back to Newry. With all that death and destruction, there was still nobody, nobody, looking out of that sub-division. And you see when you weren't there; I mean I can remember getting married and being on my honeymoon and away for three weeks. And I was sitting in Spain thinking 'the boys are on nightshift now' or 'the boys will be in the briefing room'. And I don't know if it was a case of missing them or a sense of loyalty that you should be there. But on your honeymoon?"

And somehow, amid all this chaos, Christopher and his colleagues had to try to carry out normal policing duties.

"Me and my son were cleaning out the garage one day and we came across old notebooks. And he was reading the notebooks and he says 'I can't believe this'. So I tell him to shout the date out which he does. And I'm able to say 'Yep, I remember that: Friday morning, landmine, police car hit, we were the first crew on the scene, two dead, one still alive. I ended up going in the ambulance with the two bodies to the morgue, along with a sergeant, two SOCOs and a photographer, processing the bodies, taking their personal belongings whatever off them.

"And having done that I'm told they need me to let one of the officers on guard outside the operating theatre get away. This is at Daisy Hill Hospital. And I'm there about five or ten minutes when a sergeant comes out and it's like a scene from MASH. His hands had just come out of this officer's body. He'd stabilised him long enough to get him to theatre. And he just walked out covered in blood. And he tells us this guy is now stable enough to be airlifted to the Royal [Victoria Hospital in Belfast].

"And once all that was done, it was back to the station for lunch. And my notebook simply reads 'refreshment break; 12:45pm resume mobile patrol'. And I can't remember what the next thing was but it was something like, you know, 'Mrs Smith reports two bottles of milk stolen from her doorstep'. And you go to that and you walk up the path and knock on the door. And Mrs Smith has no understanding of where you've been or what you've just done, you know, she wants her milk bottles found. That was just the way it was: a cycle of terror, death and destruction and then the road traffic accident or whatever. That was just what we lived with."

*Not his real name.

The Map

10

Split Second

"It's a hell of a thing, killing a man. Take away all he's got and all he's ever gonna have." Clint Eastwood as William Munny in Unforgiven.

"Put it down; put the gun down." Bryan* knew it was him yelling, but his voice sounded somehow different – like an echo bouncing back from somewhere outside his body, familiar and strange in the same moment.

He felt his finger on the trigger of his standard issue American-made Ruger revolver, a .357 Magnum, felt the pressure increase by the tiniest of increments. A matter of feet away, a suspected terrorist was pointing a stolen Ruger Mini-14 semi-automatic rifle at him. Bryan could feel the blood rushing through his veins. Almost imperceptibly his trigger finger moved…

Bryan was well known in the Newry area. His reputation was that of a 'tough but fair' street savvy cop. He had proved his courage on more than one occasion. Put simply, he was a professional. He knew risk was part of the job. It was something he accepted, but equally it was something he tried to minimise and mitigate against at every opportunity.

Even today, Bryan checks under his car every time he gets into it, a lesson driven home by an incident that seared its way into his memory more than forty years ago.

"We were on mobile patrol in Newry when we got a call that there had been an under car booby trap explosion. It had just gone off outside a place called the Copper Grill.

"When we got there, we found the badly damaged car and inside it were people with horrific injuries. We just couldn't get them out of it. We had to wait for the fire brigade. One of the people in the car died and two were badly injured.

"It later transpired they were members of the Territorial Army (TA) who had been working at a nearby telephone exchange. They had been targeted by the IRA who had apparently decided that TA people were what they called 'legitimate targets'.

"Even before then, I had been aware of the possibility of an under car booby trap bomb. But from that day on I checked my car all the time. I still do it and that was forty years ago. I check every morning. Even at the height of the Troubles, I always looked for somewhere to park where you could check your car without bringing attention to yourself, because, if somebody saw you checking your car, it would be obvious that you were a member of the security forces and you could have found yourself targeted as a result."

Like so many potential targets, Bryan tried, as best he could, to protect his children not only from physical harm, but also from the psychological impact that came with knowing there were people out there who wanted to kill you.

"The kids used to ask what I was doing and I would tell them I was just checking there were no cats under the car. I used to say that it was nice and warm in there for cats and that I just wanted to be sure I wouldn't run over any of them."

Sometimes, however, saving your own life can depend upon your willingness to take that of someone else, which brings us back to where this chapter started.

"When I was working in Newry, I would have been involved a lot with terrorist suspects, you know stopping them and checking them out. These people were trying to kill me so it was important that, first of all, I knew them and that I made it harder for them to kill police officers or soldiers. So I would have been regularly stopping them, checking them out, taking details off them etc. Then I would pass all of this information into the system to help Special Branch monitor their movements.

"This particular night, we were outside Newry when we spotted a car being driven by a suspect. He pulled across in front of us so we followed him up the Dublin Road out of Newry. I found it was always best to stop people outside of town where they couldn't get a crowd gathered up and maybe start a scene.

"So we got him pulled in on the hard shoulder. There were three guys in the car, all suspected terrorists. I knew the driver quite well and he knew me. But there wasn't the usual banter. I found that a bit strange. He would have been stopped so often that he sort of just accepted it and sometimes he would even have joked with you a bit. But this night he seemed edgy. I told him I was going to search him and asked him to turn around. We're trained not to have the suspect facing you during a searches, obviously, it would make it much easier for him to lash out at you with either a punch or kick. But this time he refused, telling me to 'f**k off'.

"So after a while I thought 'well, I'm going to have to search him anyway and there's no point in creating a whole scene' so I started to search him facing forwards.I was searching him from the top down and just as I got to about his waist, he suddenly kicked out, catching me under the chin and I fell back. Obviously, when something like that happens, you're all over the place. I was getting myself gathered up when one of the young constable, who was with me came running over to help, but he was tripped up by another of the suspects. He fell face down and his rifle went clattering up the road.

At this point, the first suspect grabbed the rifle and pointed it at Bryan. "I drew my revolver and I was shouting at him 'Put it down, put it down'. And I started to squeeze the trigger. I got to the first pressure point which meant it would have taken very, very little to fire the pistol. And he was looking at me with the rifle up, not all the way up into a firing position, but about halfway.. The only thing was that I knew we wouldn't normally have a round 'up the spout' in that particular rifle. I was thinking 'he has to cock it and, if he does, I'm shooting'. In my head, that was the line of no return. "And I was so, so close to shooting him. Then he just threw the rifle down and sort of smirked."

Bryan has no doubt the suspect would have been fully aware of the potential for this situation to end in the death of – at least – one of them.

"Oh, he knew I was pointing my revolver at him and he must've known that no judge would have convicted me. Was my life in immediate danger? Well, you don't get danger more immediate than a terrorist pointing a rifle at you from a few feet away.

"Naturally, there was a lot of adrenaline involved at the time. But when you get back to the station and start to settle down, that's when it hits you. I remember thinking 'Crikey, what just happened there'?"

"People might think 'ah, they're a terrorist; kill them. But you're still taking someone's life. Afterwards, when I reflected on it, I thought on how that could have changed my whole life, could've changed my family's life. If I had shot that guy – allegedly one of the top terrorists in the country at that time, that would've made me a big target for them. Realistically, I'd have had to move out of the country – to go and live somewhere else because you couldn't live with the stress and your family situation where your home could be attacked. You would always feel like you had a target on your back. I mean, within the law, I know I would have been right. A rifle was being pointed at me. My life was definitely in danger. I don't believe any judge would have said I was wrong. But the repercussions for me and my family would have been that I would have had to leave the country. People say you could have moved away to Coleraine or Bangor or wherever but I would never have felt comfortable in this country again. Terrorists could always find you if they were determined to.

*Now retired, Bryan spends much of his time living overseas.

The Map

11

White Lines

For most of a day I had stood in that cruel, freezing rain, stamping my feet on the pot-holed, muddy road in a bid to keep whatever bit of heat that remained in my body from following the rest and just leaving.

The raindrops were like little silver daggers that were blowing straight across the open fields stinging my cheeks. Another day, another South Armagh laneway, another murder attempt by the IRA.

My mind was just starting to wander, I was starting to feel a bit sorry for myself, when the sudden, insistent whirr of camera motors and a familiar little flutter of excitement dragged me back to the job in hand.

SOCOs (Scenes of Crime Officers). The press pack loved SOCOs: They wore white suits, they strode in and out of crime scenes, they carried evidence bags that screamed 'something is happening here'. In short, they offered pictures, and for journalists (TV or newspapers) pictures were food and drink.

But I'm going to let you into a little secret; there was another reason why we loved SOCOs so much: they protected us. They formed a clean, white, sterile barrier between us and the horror. By which I mean the real, messy, bloody, unfiltered, unedited horror, the not for teatime viewing, not for anytime viewing, horror.

What exactly was inside that forensic tent? What was in those evidence bags I mentioned? And what of the baggage that couldn't be set down, the emotional baggage? In a world where conditions such as PTSD (Post Traumatic Stress Disorder) were barely recognised, how did these men and women cope?

Some didn't and very quickly moved back, or on, to alternative departments. Others though developed techniques that allowed them to keep going on days when it must have seemed the carnage would never end.

For David*, it was the role that was to define the bulk of his policing career. He had a cast-iron reputation for thoroughness and a conviction record to match.

Friday, February 9, 1996, had been, for newsagent Inam Bashir, a day just like any other. Inam was a well-known character in the London Docklands with a cheery word and a smile for everyone who visited his kiosk from which he sold newspapers and sweets.

His mother, Mrs Hamida Bashir, would later tell an inquiry by the NI Affairs Committee that her son had always been a kind and generous person. Even at school, she said, it was clear to everyone the man he would grow up to be as he shared, without hesitation, his toys and sweets with fellow pupils.

"Every Friday, he would bring home fruit for me and his Dad," she said.

But not that Friday.

That Friday, Inam and his friend and colleague, John Jeffries, were blown through two solid walls by an IRA bomb, an IRA bomb that had been made in South Armagh using military-grade Semtex explosives supplied by Muammar Gaddafi's regime in Libya. The two friends were killed instantly.

The bomb contained 3,000lbs of ammonium nitrate mixed with sugar, packed into plastic sacks and wrapped around Semtex-filled 'booster tubes'. It was hidden in a specially-made compartment in a flatbed Ford Iveco lorry which had been made to look like a tow truck. An IRA man drove the bomb from South Armagh, across to GB via the Belfast to Stranraer ferry, then 300 miles south to the capital. Along the way, he left three thumbprints – one at Stranraer, one at a services area in Carlisle and one in East London. The difficulty was that, although the police believed these were the driver's prints, they couldn't put a name to them as the fingerprints did not appear anywhere in the national database. The driver had never been convicted of any offence - at that time.

David's professional reputation and knowledge of South Armagh made him the obvious choice when the Metropolitan Police came looking for a SOCO to head up the South Armagh part of their investigation. It was to be an eye-opening experience for him. "It seemed to be that money was no object," he said. "There were helicopters and planes on standby at Aldergrove shifting stuff back to labs in GB for analysis. The money they fired into that operation; as somebody who had served there for so many years, I just couldn't believe it.

"Just one example. There was a car of interest and a guy in the south had bought it. A Met officer came over and met me and we went to see this man. I don't think he could believe his luck when the officer gave him an absolute fortune for the car; at least twice what it was worth. A car transporter was then brought over from London, the car was placed on it. It was all sealed up and off it went to London again."

At one stage, David identified a phone box which he suspected had been used for making one of the telephoned warnings and it was a similar story. The phone box was lifted out in its entirety, sealed and shipped to London.

But there was also an alarming lack of knowledge of the area at times with the Met almost naïve in many ways. The lorry used in the Docklands bomb was a 'ringer', that is a stolen vehicle disguised as legitimate. David explained: "I found the chassis of the original lorry in South Armagh and I told the Met that we would have to take it out straight away due to the difficulty of holding a scene overnight where it had been found. And they just laughed at me. They said they would go back for it the following day. 'It won't be there', I told them. But they wouldn't listen. Anyway, they DID go back for it the next day and all they found was the dead grass where the chassis had been sitting."

This sort of naivety, and indeed this sort of spending, had no absolutely no place in the vast bulk of David's working life where naivety or carelessness of any sort would be paid for in lives.

"County Armagh is the smallest county in Northern Ireland but it had the most murders during the Troubles," explained David.

"So the security of all police and army personnel was paramount. Even going to the most trivial of crimes, there was a lot of security work to be done. You were depending on uniformed police to secure the area. Indeed, in a lot of areas, it was military search teams who would clear routes.

Soldiers clearing a route in South Armagh

"You also depended on military helicopters to get you out to scenes as it often wasn't safe to drive on the roads. So you spent a lot of time going to and from Bessbrook where the main helipad was at the time.

"We got to recognise different types of helicopter from the sound and I can tell you when you were out on the ground, tired, hungry, freezing cold, trying to stay alert to threats; there was no nicer sound."

David's admiration for the pilots into whose hands he and his colleagues regularly placed their lives, is clear. "There were two pilots from the Royal Marines who flew Lynx helicopters and no matter WHAT the weather was like, they would have come and got you out. Every time." Others were more circumspect on occasions where the weather closed in and from time to time, it was just a case of making do.

"Then you would just have had to bunk down behind a hedge, or – if you were close to a military tower – you would have gone there."

For David, the way through the mayhem of those days was to have a "SOCO head" and to learn to box away the stuff he saw with that head on. But it was often not quite as simple as that.

"One case that has always stuck with me was the death of a young soldier from Perth in Scotland and I think it's because I was going on holiday to Perth almost immediately after his death."

Perhaps the case, so fresh in his mind, and the unfortunate coincidence of being in the soldier's home town so soon after, allowed a little leakage from the SOCO's world into the loving family man's world. Whatever the reason, it is a case that has always stayed with David.

The victim was Graham Alexander Stewart and he was a Lance Sergeant in the Second Battalion of the Scots Guards. The rank of Lance Sergeant is uncommon now in the British Army but it is retained by the Guards regiments. Graham was 24.

David recalled: "Sergeant Stewart and three of his colleagues had been formed into what was known as a 'close observation' patrol. They were helicoptered in to an area just outside the village of Cullyhanna and had taken up a position on high ground. It was a wooded area with hedges and a lane behind them.

"As they looked down towards Cullyhanna there was a derelict building and another lane. The ground fell away at the rear of that derelict building then there was undulating ground which, unfortunately, created a blind spot for the nearby military observation post.

"Stones had been set up along the ridge at the top of this dip and in one area, they were set up like a bridge giving an effective observation hole through them or cover for using this as a firing point.

"So on the day of the killing, the IRA set up a heavy machine gun in this blind spot and fired a large number of shots up into the wooded area where the soldiers were. Unfortunately, Lance Sergeant Stewart was killed in the attack."

In listening to David recount incidents like this, you come to see how suitable he was for the job. He is calm, unflappable, professional and most definitely not prone to overstating or exaggerating events. What he describes as 'a large number' of shots fired by the IRA was actually almost two hundred.

"Obviously, Lance Sergeant Stewart and his colleagues were evacuated. I arrived at 08:30 the following morning along with the photographer and mapper. The area had been secured by other soldiers who had lain out all night.

"The first area I went to was the area where Lance Sergeant Stewart and his colleagues had been. I could see strike marks on the branches of trees. The soldiers had been well embedded but obviously their position had been compromised somehow.

"The army did return fire but didn't claim any hits. I recovered 151 spent cartridge cases and machine gun links from the area.

"There were spent cases and links at a second site (so obviously the IRA had two heavy machine guns) and spent cases at two other sites. I suspected that these had come from a Heckler and Koch G3 rifle. Heckler and Koch rifles have very distinctive fluting marks." David also found face veils that were probably used to cover the barrels of the machine guns.

But, as with most killings of this type in South Armagh, a conviction was never likely and indeed none was ever secured.

If the death of Lance Sergeant Stewart was tough to handle, there was worse in store.

"In rural areas like Armagh, everybody got to know everybody else because you were all depending on each other.

"I worked with SOCO in one of the Belfast stations before coming to Armagh and in Belfast you only really knew the boys in your own office. You didn't seem to get to know anybody else. They had a totally different way of working in Belfast whereas in rural areas CID, SOCO, Mapping, Photography worked as a team."

But there was a terrible downside to being so close to people.

"On three occasions, I had been sitting chatting to guys in the canteen literally about five minutes before they were blown up and murdered. There was one lad Reggie Williamson and he and I would have gone to the gym together every day at lunchtime or out for a run. I was at the gym with him that lunchtime and at the scene of his murder that night."

The Reserve Constable was killed when an under-car bomb exploded as he drove home after a night out in the village of Moy, just across the Armagh-Tyrone border.

"My wife was also in the police and I had to attend the murder of one of her squad mates who I knew well. Even some of the civilians who were killed you knew them because Armagh, as you well know Gordon, is a small place and you just got to know people.

"I suppose at the time when you went to a scene you just wanted to do the best you could for the victim, gather up what evidence you could. You were so busy at the scene and for days afterwards. It wasn't until everything quietened down again that you started sort of processing and trying to deal with it.

"There are times when it comes back to you. Some of these old historic cases, you put them to the back of your mind and you think you've locked that door and something brings it all back to you. You could be driving down a road and suddenly you realise 'oh, so and so was killed here'. It never really goes away you know.

"If you sit and think about all the things you had to do – people you knew blown to pieces and maybe you were gathering them up in plastic bags. But you just had to get on with it. It was some time later that it could come back on you."

*Not his real name.

The Map

12

The 'On Switch'

"It's like, when you joined the police you got switched on, but nobody ever came back to switch you off."

"You couldn't just go home, close your door and get on with a nice, ordinary life. The hyper-vigilance never left you: you know; maybe you'd see a different postman on the street where you lived and you'd be asking yourself: Who is this guy? Where's the usual postie? Is there somebody hiding along the street waiting to shoot me?'"

Avril* glances down as she stirs her second cup of tea. She purses her lips almost imperceptibly and I know she is weighing and considering her reply. In the business she is in, words matter.

We've agreed to meet in the home of one of her former clients and I am glad we have. It feels like a privilege to be a witness to the level of unshakeable trust that exists between the police officer and Avril, the one-time nurse he describes as 'the top Cognitive Behavioural Therapist specialising in troubles-related PTSD (Post Traumatic Stress Disorder). Avril has helped hundreds of police officers, members of the military and civilians.

The client is in no doubt she has saved the lives of many of those officers, including a good friend of his. He told me of how he found his friend about to take his own life at a remote location in the early hours of the morning. He brought the man home to the house we're sitting in now, and phoned Avril. She sat with the officer until the immediate crisis had passed. He was later diagnosed with PTSD and successfully treated.

There was no area in Northern Ireland where officers were as likely to encounter trauma or were as unable to switch off as that covered by 'the Map'.

The village of Newtownhamilton after an INLA car bomb. The bombers gave a very short warning and the police were still trying to clear the area when the bomb exploded.

"I don't like using the word normal because what is normal? But I do know that it's NOT normal to witness such scenes constantly," says Avril. "If it's a single incident, recovery tends to be good. But there are police officers who have experienced multiple traumas and they, often, will have chronic PTSD."

But the reality is that for police officers here, the condition was not even recognised before the mid-80s which means many older officers came through the worst years of the Troubles with nobody to turn to for help. For some, alcohol became a crutch.

"But that was a maladaptive coping mechanism," explains Avril. "It was part of a culture of drinking but then the drinking often became the main problem because obviously alcohol addiction has to be treated before you can treat any trauma."

It was in the '80s that PTSD was first recognised in the US as more and more Vietnam veterans began to develop symptoms. The sheer numbers made it impossible to ignore. But, as Avril explains, almost inevitably, things moved a lot more slowly here.

"Even as our understanding grew, it was still seen as – and I hate to use this word – a weakness. A lot of police officers would have said 'Well, I'm not going to admit that there's anything wrong with my mental health. They saw it as weakness but there was also fear. They were afraid to speak to their senior officers and the truth is that the senior officers didn't really accept it. It just wasn't talked about. The sort of the culture was 'well, you joined the police. You knew what you were getting into'."

Another murder, another lonely road. Danger was ever present for police officers and soldiers in South Armagh.

In the mid-90s, there was some change, at least in the approach and attitude of the RUC to mental health. It followed very public criticism of the system of care within the force as it existed at that time.

On February 4, 1992, a police officer called Allen Moore had shot dead three people in Sinn Fein's office on the Falls Road in Belfast before killing himself with the same weapon, his own legally-held shotgun. His Ruger revolver had been taken from him the previous day after he had fired shots over a dead colleague's grave. It soon became clear that Const Moore had a very complex set of psychological problems.

The RUC had created an occupational health unit six years earlier. It was staffed by two doctors and two specialist nurses, but the Coroner told the inquest into Const Moore's death that the unit's approach to stress management within the RUC was "underdeveloped compared to other police forces".

The same inquest heard the force's suicide rate described as "a disgrace". Constable Moore's death at his own hand was one of at least fifty seven such deaths between 1978 and 1993. That this period was also among the worst years of the 'Troubles' is surely more than mere coincidence.

"The high prevalence of suicide among police officers was due to a lot of factors," says Avril. "I think it was the shame and embarrassment. It was so much easier to go in and to say 'look, I've been shot in the leg' than to say your mental health was suffering.

"A lot of police would have suffered in silence and they had access to firearms and they could use those firearms to end their life and sadly quite a lot of them did."

She says many, if not most, would not even have recognised the symptoms.

"A lot of people would have ended up just going to their GP and maybe being diagnosed with anxiety or depression. Other symptoms can include sleep disturbance, nightmares, hyper-vigilance, anger and irritability."

Avril is a warm and caring, person and it is instantly clear that the years she gave to trying to help people affected by debilitating conditions such as PTSD meant much more to her than simply work. It will never be possible to put a figure on it, but there are police officers walking around today who owe Avril and those like her their lives.

*Not her real name.

The Map

13

The Price Of Peace Is Eternal Vigilance

Constable Andy Mawhinney stood on a low wall, watching the lonely figure of the Ammunition Technical Officer (ATO), silhouetted against the light. The soldier looked bulky, awkward and slow in his blast-resistant suit. But speed was not the priority here. ATOs are highly trained professionals. The soldier knew many lives, not least his own, depended on his approach to this task. Methodically, painstakingly, he went through the process of checking the petrol tanker for booby traps.

The tanker had been stolen two days earlier. Andy and his colleagues were confident they knew exactly who had taken it – a high profile republican - and equally confident that he and his gang wouldn't have left the now-empty tanker without at least one 'surprise'.

"Normally, petrol tankers wouldn't go any further south than Ford's Cross," explained Andy. "Beyond that line they would have needed aerial support. But, for some reason, on this particular occasion, it went without aerial support and, perhaps not surprisingly, it was hijacked. We received intelligence that suggested it could be found not far from a farm owned by the man we suspected of having taken it."

The farm complex straddled the border between Northern Ireland and the Republic of Ireland near a place called Glassdrummond.

Andy recalled: "He had pipes in the north which fed into tanks in the south, literally only about 50m away."

If South Armagh was difficult and dangerous to police then it was at its most dangerous and its most difficult right here. Between 50 and 100 soldiers and police officers would have been involved in the operation, initially to sweep and clear the area, and then to secure it. Garda and Irish army support would also have been in place just across the border.

The ATO had first cleared the cab of the lorry.
"Then he climbed on top of the tanker. He started to open the hatches. He tied a pull cord around each hatch in turn than retired to a safe distance from where he would simply flip the hatch open with the cord.
"Then he would go back up and repeat the procedure until he came to the last one. Again he came back down and pulled the cord. The next thing there was this massive blast. The shock wave went up through the trees and we all looked at it in awe for a few moments."
Then, slowly at first, little thumps began to be heard. Then more, and more……. and then many more.
"They were dead crows falling out of the trees," explained Andy. "I mean, the place was covered in them.

It was so surreal. All we could do was stare. It was like something out of a Hollywood movie."

The truth was that, no matter how bizarre it may have seemed, for young men and women like Andy, this was simply the job for which they had signed up; where the abnormal could, it seemed, slide seamlessly into the completely normal. But it was a job loved by the vast majority of them, a job with a camaraderie and a sense of purpose which they would never find again.

"I joined the police in 1980. I went down to the depot on a Sunday afternoon, got dropped off by the folks. I had an interest in the outdoor pursuit type of thing and community policing. Going through the training centre, the first half was great; second half we got moved up to be the senior squad and we all got blown up coming back from the swimming pool. Then near the end of our training…"

Woah. Hang on a second. In fact, let's back it up a bit.

Andy had just casually dropped in that line about getting blown up on the way back from the swimming pool with no more concern or excitement in his voice than if he'd been telling me how he'd bagged his 50-metre distance badge.

"Your squad was blown up on the way back from the swimming pool?"

"At that stage in the training centre, physical fitness was one of the big things and once a week you would go swimming over at the forum. It was the routine; everyone went swimming and you all marched across in order. You wore a shirt and tie and a jacket. It was all very formal.

"Anyway, this particular day, we were coming back to the depot across a car park and there was a car parked up beside a building.

"We all walked past it; by pure fluke the majority of the squad got past safely. Next minute, the vehicle exploded and four or five of the squad were injured. But thankfully not seriously. The rest of us ran back to help and didn't think anything of it.

"The people who had been detonating the bomb couldn't see their main target. They had to assume where we were and thankfully most of us were already past the car. The blast itself went down into the boggy ground around the forum and then up as opposed to around and out which is what would've happened on harder ground."

Bearing in mind that these were mostly teenagers, you might have expected a few to walk away from their chosen career.

"But you know something; there wasn't anybody in the squad who wanted to quit – I mean you hear about officers currently, because of the increased threat, turning round and saying 'the job's not for me, I'm going to leave'. Well that just never happened."

Soon, Andy found himself on his way to the area covered by 'The Map'.

"Straight after the training depot, I was sent to Castlereagh to do a driving course. Afterwards, a Chief Inspector came in to tell me that I was going to the old 'H' Division. I'll never forget hm looking up at me and saying 'Ah; Constable Mawhinney; I see you're leaving the RUC………. and joining the Newry Police Force'. It was a joke, of course, but one which, as I was to quickly discover, had a lot of truth in it."

Things were indeed done differently in 'H' Division.

"Right from the start, I wanted to go out with the military patrols as it got me out of the routine of ordinary police work and got me flying in helicopters and doing stuff that you would have paid a fortune to do in civilian life.

Constable Andy Mawhinney with some of the Royal Marines whose professionalism, he says, saved lives.

"It really was something for a 20-year-old, fresh out of the depot. I was flying in helicopters, carrying a gun, landing, walking over fields and it was great. All the heli-patrols that you did, I mean, they weren't on the Banbridge side of Newry; they were all in around Killeen, the Omeath Road, across towards Camlough and Meigh. Not as far as Forkhill but right on the border. We couldn't patrol that area in cars but we were able to do it in helicopters with military support. And yes, there was a threat there continually but, while you were aware of it, it didn't ever make you apprehensive to the point where you didn't want to go out on the ground."

He does, however, concede that you had to keep your wits about you at ALL times.

The Permanent Vehicle Check Point (PVCP) at Cloghohue near Newry

"The IRA was by no means a shabby organisation. As much as I hate to say it, they were about as professional as you were going to get at that stage. They were a force to be reckoned with. Especially in South Armagh. They had the logistics around them. They knew what they were doing. They watched and came to understand what the security forces were doing.

"Even booby trapping things like flags up telegraph poles. They knew they had been taken down before so they thought it would be done again. And they saw where you put cordons in place. The first thing that you did if you were the security forces was you observed the area. If you were out on patrol and walking through fields towards a gate, you were checking around the gate. Even when you were walking towards culverts – we had a system in place where you came in towards the culvert but you fanned out round it and the furthest point in the spread of the officers or military was there to try to identify any command wires. So you were always looking as you approached things. And it wasn't just normally walking the fields. You were checking high ground, you were watching vehicles approaching, you were conscious of vans, you were conscious of lorries. And you knew as you patrolled certain areas where attacks had taken place; that ambushes happen in areas that are best-placed to suit the ambushers. So, if there had been attacks there before, there might be again at the same spot. So you were always aware, always alert.

"And you had to try to respond differently. The problem with South Armagh, though, be it Newry Sub-Division or Crossmaglen is that it is not a big area. And going back to where best-placed ambushes happen, it is because the person carrying out the ambush expects success.

"So they had the advantage to some extent. I mean, if you think about Ford's Cross where you had the helicopter shoots; there was always the one spot where they put the gun team – and that was on the high ground on a route which they knew the helicopters would take. And when you were flying out of Bessbrook towards Crossmaglen the majority of pilots just followed the roads. So as soon as you flew out of Bessbrook you turned out over Camlough lake, then you bounced onto the main Newry Road through Ford's Cross and down over Creggan. As you were approaching Crossmaglen, you broke left over the chapel and you always came in from the Lismore Estate end to the helipad. And that was the route and you thought nothing of it."

Like most officers who served in South Armagh, Andy quickly became knowledgeable about helicopters – and pilots.

"There was one pilot from the Royal Marines who always flew Gazelles and, if you were lucky enough to get picked up by him, either on your own or maybe with one other officer, he would skim the water on Camlough Lake. You couldn't pay for that now and, even if you could, sure health and safety no doubt would ruin it."

While Andy did not underestimate the IRA's capability – and indeed their willingness to kill - he does believe that the discipline of his colleagues and the military helped them avoid even heavier casualties.

"If you look at the way the majority of terrorist incidents happened and, with the exception of the so-called border sniper, it was always shots fired en masse.

"The terrorists basically wanted to put down as many rounds as possible and to hope for, as they would see it, a success ie; to hit and kill a police officer or a soldier. I remember going to scenes and the amount of spent cases and no hits it was amazing.

"I'm not saying the terrorists didn't have training but maybe because of a lack of discipline thankfully they didn't have the success they perhaps could have."

But the threat was always there. As every military patrol that left Crossmaglen station had at least one police officer with it and every officer knew there was a risk of coming under fire.

Andy recalls one such incident. "On this particular day, there were two police officers and it was twelve soldiers, maybe sixteen but I think it was 12 because I remember we were dropped off by a Wessex [helicopter] and I think they could only take fourteen or sixteen max so it sort of worked out that you had three 'bricks' of four soldiers and two police officers. The other police officer had just arrived in Crossmaglen about a week earlier and this was one of his first patrols. Normally, the more experienced officer would be in the lead brick and your patrol would be the first to come across any cars to stop or to speak with members of the public.

Graffiti in Crossmaglen

But on this particular occasion, we got dropped off at Glassdrummond and the new officer opted to go in the first brick and I went with the second brick. We'd just come off the main Glassdrummond Road and we broke right on to the Leeter Road towards Mounthill Road. We were walking ON the actual road and we were spread out. There was the first brick of four soldiers and the one police officer. We were about fifty metres behind them and the third brick was about the same distance behind us. We were making our way towards some high ground and the next minute shots were fired. The first thing you heard was "contact, contact, wait out" closely followed by the instruction 'watch my tracer'."

Tracer rounds are bullets with small pyrotechnic charges built into them. When fired, the charge burns extremely brightly making the path of the round visible. The first soldier who believed he knew where the enemy shots had come from would fire a tracer round for his comrades to see and follow.

"Suddenly, there were shots being fired by the military all round you, but by this stage, the young police officer in the first brick had fallen to the ground. I went forward to him and found he'd been shot in the arm, hit in the bicep actually with a .762 round fired from a high-powered, bolt action Gerand rifle.

"He needed medical attention and we patched him up to control the bleeding. Once we knew the situation was under control, a Wessex helicopter was flown in. Myself, the injured officer and a medic, who was already on board having come from Bessbrook, all flew straight to Belfast to Musgrave Park Hospital where we handed my injured colleague over to the military doctors then flew back to Bessbrook. Somebody brought my jacket and car keys to me and I went on home. I remember the Chief [Inspector] phoned me to ask if I needed a couple of days off but I just said 'no thanks, I'm happy enough'.

"So he said instead he would send me, kind of for a spot of R and R, over to England for NITAT (Northern Ireland Terrorist Awareness Training). So myself and a sergeant from Forkhill flew to Heathrow where we were picked up in a short-wheelbase, canvas top, army Land Rover. The sergeant sat in the front with the driver while I got the back which, I can tell you, it was a bumpy run all the way to where the training was being given. At that stage the army regiment going through was 40 Commando Royal Marines who had just come back from the Falklands. They were going into South Armagh for their first operational tour back in the UK. So I had to act as a police officer would in South Armagh and help to train these soldiers who were coming across; to give them an idea of how to behave and what was expected of the 'green army' support to the police.

"And the irony was that the first scenario we were all tasked to respond to was a sniper attack – and this was our so-called R and R! The Royal Marines were brilliant and it meant that I got to know some of them before they even got to Crossmaglen which was good. Without a doubt, their professionalism when on the ground in South Armagh saved lives."

The ingenuity of the IRA, particularly its bomb makers, also meant constant vigilance was required on the part of the security forces. Andy hands me a photo of a cow blown apart when it tripped a booby trap bomb.

"That cow actually detonated a booby trap and that's why we went out to the scene, but when we got there, we discovered there was an additional booby trap. Our plan was to clear the area and bring in a SOCO. But ATO found the second one.

"The way the terrorists worked, the second device would be left in a spot where they knew the military would set up as part of their response."

At these times, local knowledge would prove invaluable and Andy says, despite everything, people around Crossmaglen WERE willing to help.

The grisly remains of a cow that detonated a booby trap bomb

"Whenever a bomb went off in the area, we could simply phone people who lived nearby to where we thought the blast was and ask them 'Has a bomb gone off down your way?' and they – 100 per cent of the time – would tell us, you know, 'Yeh, there was a blast down here; it rattled our windows' or whatever. And it meant when you were giving the handover briefing that night or the following day, the area could be overflown by helicopter and you were able to narrow down the search area and that was because we had the opportunity to tap into local knowledge, knowing there were people there who would pick up the phone and talk to you."

This type of methodical approach undoubtedly helped preserve the lives of Andy and his colleagues.

"I thoroughly enjoyed getting up to go to work every day. There were days where I didn't enjoy the sights and experience of the day but you went back home that night, went to bed, got up in the morning and back to work. And nobody that I knew and worked with at that time had any desire not to be police officers."

He does, however, recognise the terrible price paid by so many, on whom the mental and physical toll was so severe.

"I have friends who have suffered PTSD, who have had help and have come back better people for it. You can't turn round and say someone is weaker because they've had it. The fact is they've probably been braver because they've put their hand up and said 'I need help.' For Andy, just like all his fellow officers, the risk did not go away when he took off the uniform.

"I never lost a colleague in Crossmaglen, thankfully. I did lose a colleague in Newry. I was nineteen. He was a part-time reserve man, an elderly farmer, and he was shot off duty I helped to carry his coffin which was, without doubt, a challenging task."

In the early 1980s Eamon Collins had been arrested and interviewed. For Andy, the result was a visit from Special Branch. "They had information that the IRA had been looking at me. They knew what car I was driving, they knew that I was friendly with a local girl and they knew where she worked and lived. They knew where we would go for a drink just outside Newry and they knew the route that I would take home. As it turned out their intelligence was out of date. I had changed my car about six months earlier but it was still the case that they were clearly aware of me and aware of my movements. Collins mentioned this in a chapter of his book.

"This was the first of many threats I was to receive but I guess it's a bit harder to cope with as a young officer. Still, you just do what you've been trained to do and make the necessary security arrangements and you just get on."

The Map

14

Ghosts

January '24

More than a year has passed since I was first given a copy of the map. Winter is here and an icy breeze is rattling through the skeleton-like remains of Bessbrook Mill.

The remains of Bessbrook Mill January 2024
- Photo: Greg Haire

The wind seems to find its way into every hidden corner, offering nothing by way of shelter for the little group who are picking their way through the broken glass and vast pools of rainwater.

In front is John Davis. He has been looking after the mill - or at least trying to - since the security forces left.

But it is like trying to hold back the tide; recent years have not been kind to Bessbrook Mill.

Pigeons in the rafters, watch - with bobbing heads and bright eyes - as, far below, the four men pass the armoury, the chapel, the cinema, the officers' mess. Often, the only light is the beam from John's torch. It tunnels its way through the blackness, and the little group follows it further and further, down into the centre of the once formidable fortress. Suddenly, the man walking behind John steps forward. "There," he says. "That was my office." More than two decades have passed since the man last stood in this room, but the memories are everywhere. "This was my military counterpart's office." Without even realising that he has done it, out of habit alone, he raps gently and respectfully on the door. You almost imagine you can hear an educated voice, so clearly used to giving commands, shout 'Enter!' But no, the Colonel is long gone. Just like the hundreds of young soldiers. Their voices too are easy to imagine as you pass through the accommodation block. No place here for the Colonel's quiet confidence of command. This is louder, less cultivated, harder. Young men, only beginning to make their way in life, aching to be heard; laughing, shouting, bantering; squeezing, shoulder to shoulder into the base's cinema or bar: full of life. But some are already marked for death.

For the retired police officer, that thought dominates all others. The soldiers' bedrooms, the showers: "Some poor young soldier probably had his last shower in there, went out on patrol, never came back."

Army helicopter over Bessbrook Mill

The remaining two people in this little group are myself and this book's graphic designer Greg Haire.

This site is vast, atmospheric and fascinating. But one room interests me more than all the others. "This was it," the police officer explains. The map board is still in place. John's torchlight picks it out. The map itself is gone- apparently held now in the RUC museum. But the board remains. There is a sadness about the officer. "You ok?", I ask.

The Author standing in the operations room deep inside Besbrook Mill. The board you can see housed The Map

"Y'know," he says, "there was a huge sheet of Perspex covering the map back then. I was just thinking about how often it had to be removed, then re-fitted after yet another dot was added. It's just terrible to think about it now."

Perhaps surprisingly, two items have survived; black curtains. They are mounted on rollers above the map board. "They were for use when visitors were in the area," explained the former officer. "We just rolled them down to cover the map. It was a simple, but effective, way of keeping secret plans secret."

He tells us who occupied each desk; the Colonel here, a military radio operator there; in a small office at the end of the corridor sat the SAS LO (liaison officer). He was usually a younger, less experienced member of the secretive special forces regiment who was the conduit between the operatives out on the ground, often living deep under cover, and the real world.

The Mill's use as a security installation is, like the Troubles that necessitated it, becoming the stuff of history.

A specially constructed blast wall at Bessbrook Mill which is now a listed structure - Photo: Greg Haire

But what use is history if we fail to realise that it is, in fact, our-story? That it belongs to each and every one of us. What point the sacrifices and the pain if we fail to learn from them? Where will we find forgiveness if we squander even the smallest opportunity to build a brighter future for the coming generations; to say to them 'no, it does NOT have to be like this'.

The American writer William Faulkner said: "The past is not dead; it's not even past."

We age, we forget, we think that we move on. But for so many of us the time of the Troubles will always be the indelible stain, spreading like blood from a bullet wound, time and again, across the crisp, clean white shirt of our lives. The wound is there, the stain is there. These things cannot be undone.

But thanks to the sacrifice of men and women like those I have met and written about here all was not lost. When the shooting stopped, we still had good will and good people; people who wanted, and still want, to reach out to their neighbours, not with the closed fist of hate but with the open hand of friendship.

They do that now in the space created by the courage and sacrifice of a previous generation, a generation that is starting to disappear but one that will live long in the memory.

The wall inside Besbrook Mill that displayed the details of the Security Forces whio served in the base during Operation Banner 1969 - 2007.

Photo: John Davis

The Author at Bessbrook Mill, no longer an Army base.

THE MAP

Bibliography

Collins, Eamon: Killing Rage. Granta Books, June 1998

Feeney, Brian; Kelters Seamus; McKittrick, David; McVea, David; Thornton, Chris: Lost Lives. Mainstream Publishing Company (Edinburgh) Ltd, 2001.

Harnden, Toby: Bandit Country, the IRA and South Armagh. Hodder and Stoughton, 1999.

Herman, Sir John; Holding the Line. Gill and McMillan Ltd, 1997

Maloney, Ed: A Secret History of the IRA. Penguin Books, 2002.